# A SENSE OF ASHER

**HERBERT L. FRED, M.D.**

RICHARD ASHER

# A SENSE OF ASHER
## *A new miscellany*

RICHARD ASHER

selected and introduced by
RUTH HOLLAND

Published by the British Medical Association
Tavistock Square, London WC1H 9JR

© The estate of Richard Asher

ISBN 0 7279 0136 2

First published in 1983 by the Keynes Press
in a limited edition of 300

Paperback edition 1984 British Medical Association

Reprinted 1984
Reprinted 1985
Reprinted 1987
Reprinted 1989

Printed in Great Britain by
Latimer Trend & Company Ltd, Plymouth

# Contents

# Introduction

"Dr Richard Asher, who is never dull" – *The Spectator*

"I know of no one who can debunk more pithily the sententiousness of the pompous in our profession." – Lord Cohen of Birkenhead

Richard Asher was fond of quoting Marie Lloyd's "A little of what you fancy," and supporting acts when she topped the bill must have felt like I do offering an introduction to this selection of his writings – a bit sweaty about the palms with the sense of being not what the public has paid its money for. You have, after all, only to turn to page 1 and read on to realise that Asher is a writer of outstanding quality, so you don't need me to tell you; but, like Pooh-Bah, I cannot refrain from putting my oar in and, in the belief that most pleasures are better for sharing, trying to convey something of the delights to be found in reading this "individualist of individualists."

Come to think of it, I can't lose. If you go to a party and take with you a companion who is amusing, articulate, intelligent, inspiring, and original nobody is going to complain if they have already met – they will simply greet him gladly. But anyone unacquainted with him may be glad of a few muttered words in the ear about Dr Asher while he waits behind, modestly disclaiming his own gifts: ". . . I am not a particularly good author . . . I admit that I can write, but I am not particularly proud of it . . ."

I talk of him as a friend, but I never knew him, nor am I in his profession. I make no apologies for this, since in literature time and distance mean nothing: you can meet the dead just as happily as the living, and they will take you into their confidence, tell you their jokes, give you the benefit of their opinions and experience, and ask for nothing in return but your eye on the book. What's more, as the times become so barbarous that the Goths and Vandals are at the gates trying to get out you could have more chance of finding civilised companions in print than in the flesh and all-too-frequently-spilled blood. Of course, the personality that comes over on the page might not be the same as the everyday one – Milton, for instance, according to his latest biographer, was rather a jolly soul, which you'd hardly gather from *Paradise Lost* or *Areopagitica* – but I suspect that in Asher's case they are not so very dissimilar. He was, according to those who knew him, a delightful companion; a happy family man; a skilled musician and craftsman; witty, playful, and eccentric; "a pastmaster of the un-expected"; a fellow, in fact, of infinite jest, of most excellent fancy; and that is how he wrote. Even his most serious and weighty articles sparkle with sequins – his own aphorisms, imaginary dialogue, fantasies, quotations – and he had that knack of being always entertaining, which Shaw described as having your pockets stuffed with sausages and keeping a red hot poker in the fire.

To begin at the beginning: Richard Asher was born in Nottingham in 1912, the son of a clergyman, and was educated at Lancing College and the London Hospital, qualifying in 1935. He was appointed physician to the Central Middlesex Hospital in 1943, and in the same year married a musician, Margaret Eliot; they had three children, Peter, Jane, and Clare. He remained at the Central Middlesex Hospital until 1964, having become senior physician in 1948.

His first published material appeared around 1940. An

article on "The treatment of tired heart" in *Medical Press and Circular* was accompanied by the following rather wary comment from the editor: "A request for an article on 'Tired Heart' produced this amusing, if somewhat flippant, contribution. We publish it because anything which brings a smile to the face in these 'grim but gay' days is to be welcomed." Already Asher's characteristic no nonsense approach is evident, combined with his gift for a telling phrase: "Just as many people who disapprove of drinking fly to the solace of invalid port because of their desire for alcohol, so do thousands who disapprove of laziness take refuge with their tired hearts because of their desire for inactivity." "The treatment is long, tedious, and lucrative."

From 1943 he contributed as one of the anonymous "peripatetic correspondents" to the *Lancet*'s "In England Now" column, and his pieces vary in quality from the brilliant to the near miss and the leaden. But very quickly he found his feet as a writer, and in February 1943 his first major article appeared in the *Lancet*. Its title was "Medicine and meaning," and, as so often, Asher was ahead of his time. Nowadays, just as nobody rips the fields to ribbons with a motorway without saying they're improving the environment, so it has become rather the thing to talk about saving the English language, even among those busy spitting out its mangled remains, such as television reporters and Sunday journalists, but it was hardly one of the prevailing winds of opinion in 1943. The piece opens with a couple of sentences that immediately catch the eye (even if the first is stretching a point – or rather, a digit): "Man is superior to the higher apes not only in opposing his thumbs but in the using of symbols, mostly spoken or written words, to convey his meaning. But the power of words has increased till they have become tyrants interfering with the transmission of ideas and of knowledge." Typically practical, Asher argues that language should be handled carefully not for its own sake but because when badly used it gets in the way of clear thinking: you can't have precision of thought without precision in language, and vice versa. Examples, as Dr Johnson said, are more efficacious than precept, and Asher's own articles are a happy instance of the medium for once really being the message: good writing about good writing. If language is, as he said, a vehicle by which thought can travel, his own thought always travelled first class, and one of his greatest gifts to medicine was to set such a very high standard in medical writing.

Asher tended to make light of this achievement, cheerfully scrawling graffiti over his own pedestal by declaring, "The standard of medical writing is so low that a doctor literate enough to put on paper something that can be read and understood without much suffering is soon looked on as a literary giant of cultured scholarship." But despite this becoming self deprecation he knew he was good, and many people outside medicine knew it too. Writers for the lay press were quick to take up his ideas, for his striking expression of them made ideal copy. He appealed equally to the heavies and the tabloids and his name appears in, among others, the *Daily Telegraph*, the *Sunday Times*, the *Daily Mirror*, the *Guardian*, the *Daily Mail*, the *Marylebone Mercury*, the *Evening News*, *Reveille*, the *Sunday Mirror*, the *Omaha Herald*, the *New York Herald Tribune*, the *Sun* (of Australia), and the *Terre Haute Indiana Star*. Cassandra, of the *Mirror*, used Asher's concern with language and meaning as the starting point of an article of his own on the subject ("In my capacity as President of the Society for the Prevention of Cruelty to Words I am indebted to Dr Richard Asher . . .").

To the professional journalists Asher was clearly one of the boys, and though he implied that writing was only a hobby, his approach to it was not that of the dilettante but the hard bitten weariness of the pro: "I have often thought while trying to write an article, 'Why am I doing this tedious and unrewarding thing?'" "Writing is done more by toil than gift. Is it worth it? I don't really think it is." He wrote and rewrote, scratching out words, reinserting phrases from separate scraps of paper, and throwing screwed up pages into the wastepaper basket in true Grub Street fashion. (Odd irrelevant notes crept in – the handwritten draft of an article on "The body as a machine" bears a reminder to be at the Essoldo, King's Road, at 4.30.) He worked long and hard "because I am incapable of producing anything worth reading except by a laborious process," and the superbly polished results are proof again, if any were needed, of the truth of C E Montague's maxim: Easy reading, hard writing.

Such an infinite capacity for taking pains is often cited as an attribute of genius, and Asher also had a negative quality which belongs to it – a lack of snobbery about little things. It is easy if you are very clever to become grand and think some matters beneath your notice and some skills too trivial for you to acquire, but he never fell into this trap. Gifted as a writer, he still constantly referred to Gowers's *Plain Words* and Fowler's *Modern English Usage*; he took the trouble to write a neat and legible script, kept a notebook in which he recorded interesting facts and ideas as they occurred, and taught himself to type; as a consultant he didn't forget that people other than doctors matter in medicine, pointing out that porters, ward orderlies, and telephone operators play a far more important part in a hospital than sophisticated electronic equipment, and encouraging all the hospital staff to contribute to the *Central Middlesex Hospital Magazine*, which he edited; as a physician he noticed his patients' clothes and faces and pondered their chance remarks.

All this helped to make him a superb diagnostician, and

his clinical articles, written in a personal, informal style, come across simply as the expert observations of "a physician more at home at the bedside than in the laboratory" (which is how he described himself), never being reminiscent – as others so often are – of the philosophers of Laputa, though there is sometimes a touch of Sherlock Holmes nosing out the truth from among the red herrings. Asher, like Holmes, solved a lot of problems by using common sense (which he defined as "the capacity to see the obvious even amid confusion"), and it is interesting that the writers to whom he most often refers are all very English and commonsensical: Kipling, Trollope, Jane Austen, and W S Gilbert, whose jester Jack Point's advice Asher seems to have had in mind when putting across his clinical findings:

> When they're offered to the world in merry guise,
> Unpleasant truths are swallowed with a will –
> For he who'd make his fellow creatures wise
> Should always gild the philosophic pill!

Most truths taste unpleasant after a bland diet of predigested opinion, but Asher managed to get several valuable new pills down the collective throat of his profession. It was his article on "The dangers of going to bed" that put an end to the hallowed tradition of prolonged bed rest, to the great benefit of patients. In an age increasingly eager to seek psychological causes for physical disease he produced several important contributions on the physical basis of mental illness, including the paper of that title and "Myxoedematous madness," in which he described 13 of his own patients with confusion caused by myxoedema, 10 of whom had been admitted to hospital under the Lunacy Act. The term myxoedematous madness is now an indispensable coin of medical currency, as is the Munchausen syndrome, Asher's inspired choice of name for the extraordinary desire of some people to undergo unnecessary operations and their fabrication of tall stories of baroque complexity to achieve this end.[1]

Asher's interest in the borderline between physical and mental illness was the result of his being in charge of the mental observation ward at the Central Middlesex Hospital. As well as being the basis of some of his most outstanding work this was to be also the cause of the abrupt ending of his career as a physician when, in 1964, the powers that be decreed that the ward should be taken over by a psychiatrist. Most of us, perhaps, would have put up with it for the sake of peace and settled for what we could get. Asher, with dark and splendid defiance, immediately resigned all his posts and, like Coriolanus, turned his back in scorn to find "a world elsewhere." Alas, it was not much of a world, and he died five years later.

I have touched on only some of the great variety of material that he left behind. A man who could turn his hand to virtually anything – photography, glazing, cementing floors, even the design of a decimal piano (with 10 note sequences instead of octaves) – Asher carried this versatility into medical practice, interesting himself in haematology; endocrinology; mundane things such as tapeworms, painful tongue, burning feet, and backache; and in hypnosis, which he often used successfully. He was also quick to see the growing importance of statistics and computers in medicine, speaking up for statisticians ("they have as much charm and display as much sympathy as anyone else") and expressing cogent reservations about computers. "Even if you own a computer," he pointed out, "it is advisable to spend a certain amount of time in thought." Asher had deliberately trained his powers of reasoning, and it bothered him that computers might be used as a substitute for thinking, particularly as

[1] Avery Jones F, ed. *Richard Asher talking sense*. London: Pitman Medical, 1972.

they can do only what they are told, whereas the human brain's unconscious does all sorts of things the conscious brain hasn't got the sense to ask for. His description of this in himself is endearing:

> I compare the place where my unconscious reasoning takes place to an oven, and my conscious processes to a rather harassed chef peering into it at frequent intervals to see if any dish worth while is likely to come out of it; moreover, an inferior chef, who uses processed peas and ready made cake-mixtures, and who knows that much that comes out of the oven is half-baked.

From the products of that harassed chef's oven I have chosen here a mixed hors d'oeuvre ("In England then"); several sustaining meat dishes ("Apriority," "The physical basis of mental illness," "The use of statistics in medicine," "Intracranial and extracranial computers"); some wholesome bread ("A case of health"); several bonnes bouches, both sweet and sharp; and something to make your head spin – Asher's calculation of the Snark's dinner time. The final article is called "Why are medical journals so dull?" and the short answer to that these days could be because he isn't writing for them and, as he put it, "it is inevitable that editors have to accept a certain amount of junk." But for 25 years some editors were lucky: in their pages, like MacNeice's cat, Richard Asher lurked and fizzed.

Now, at last, I'll get out of the way and let you shake his hand.

RUTH HOLLAND

xiv

# Acknowledgements

I thank Mrs Margaret Asher for kindly allowing me access to Richard Asher's papers; the editors of many medical journals, especially the *Lancet*, for permission to reprint articles originally published by them; Mr Michael Harmer, Bellman of the Snark Club, for drawing my attention to the matter of the Snark's watch; Mr D St P Barnard for supplying me with a copy of the braintwister puzzle and for allowing me to reprint this and his letter; and Mr C J Griffith Davies for explaining, and almost making me understand, the mathematical calculations.

# I

## In England then

In 1939, shortly after the outbreak of the second world war, the *Lancet* started to publish a page of anonymous items on general and medical topics called ". . . In England – Now." (Thus punctuated it is a quotation from Browning, but by 1940 austerity had blacked out poetic allusion, and from then on it was "In England Now.") Topical in the 1940s, Asher's contributions have kept fresh with their varnish of wit. The titles are mine, so no blame can be attached to him or to the *Lancet*.

## Something appealing, something appalling

Before the war, we who insure ourselves for medical protection received every year a brochure cataloguing the atrocities of our colleagues. One of the minor tragedies of the war is that we no longer receive these stimulating and cheering pamphlets. Nearly everyone has secret fears of incompetence, and the strengthening effect of reading of doctors who are even more unconscientious and incompetent than ourselves is beyond measure. How eagerly I used to await the little booklet. How enthralled I was to learn of an anonymous villain (euphemistically called "Your Member") and the unbelievable things he had done. Though at times my heart would bleed for the hapless patients of Your

Member, it would fill with rapture as I thought: "I don't believe even I would have done that!" "Your Member," I would read, "after refusing to see an accident case for a week, when he finally did see the case failed to observe three compound fractures, stating the patient's condition was due to nerves, although he was deeply unconscious. When the fractures were pointed out to him he put both elbows in a tight plaster in full flexion. At a later visit both arms were found to be gangrenous, and Your Member, considering there was some inflammation, injected 3 g of sulphapyridine. This was given subcutaneously and resulted in a considerable degree of sloughing." The story usually ended with the polite summary: "It was decided that Your Member had committed an error of judgment."

That such stories should have tonic properties is quite understandable. The normal person cannot believe he is doing all right unless he knows that someone else is doing all wrong.

## Pin back your lugholes

Somebody commented the other day that when the flying bombs were endemic in the sky the average citizen looked not drawn with anxiety or suspense but rather more vacant and fatuous than usual. I think I know the reason. Observe a friend listening to a watch. If there is difficulty in hearing the tick a sudden change comes over his face – the jaw drops, the face muscles relax, and an expression of saintly idiocy replaces that of ordinary awareness. When a Bell's palsy turned up in outpatients bitterly complaining of the classic hyperacusis, I suddenly saw the connection. Of course, relaxation of the stapedius makes you hear better, whether achieved by voluntary relaxation of all the face muscles or an involuntary palsy of the seventh nerve. This seems so

2

simple and obvious a truth it is odd that neurological textbooks make no comment. Try listening intently for a faint sound (a) with a relaxed fatuous expression and (b) with any violent grimace, and you will see that this is so. Odd that Darwin didn't comment on it in his delightful book *The Expression of Emotions in Man and Animals*, where he mentions the physical changes associated when the various senses are used. Anyway, even if you aren't convinced, I believe that the placid vacancy of London citizens was due to their relaxing not their vigilance but their stapedius muscles. A dog will prick up its ears to catch a sound. A man will prick down his face.

## One auspicious and one dropping

Here are two ways of teaching the important fact that scurvy may mimic osteomyelitis.

(1) *Suet pudding* – When due consideration is paid to the aetiological factors concerned, it is far from infrequently observed that the subperiosteal haematoma formation occurring as an integral manifestation of the scorbutic state may lead to an erroneous diagnosis of an osteomyelitic condition and thus engender as resultants both unnecessary surgical intervention and the unfortunate deprivation of the requisite ascorbic acid therapeusis.

(2) *Aperitif* – (How I was taught by Donald Hunter) – The other day I went to see a child in a surgical ward. She had pain in her shin. The surgeons stood round sharpening their knives. I was just in time. I shouted "Stop! Give her some orange juice."

## Why did the chicken . . .

This is only a preliminary communication because my mother stopped further experiments, saying it might stop the hens laying. Nevertheless, I can say that it really works – this witchcraft business of immobilising hens with their beaks on a chalk line, I mean.

*Experiment 1* – I placed a hen with its beak on a chalk line (jolly difficult, I can tell you), and on letting go gradually the hen stayed there, nose to the line (looking a most frightful ass), until after half a minute she gradually raised her head about two inches off the ground; then the spell snapped and she was off with a squawk. I repeated this several times with consistent success.

*Experiment 2* – I repeated experiment 1 but without a chalk line. No success at all. The hen was abusive and violent and escaped rapidly.

*Experiment 3* – I used white tape pinned on the lawn. Hens might like the smell of chalk because of calcium deficiency or something, but it can't be that because white tape works, if anything better.

One odd thing I noticed. There were naturally a few white feathers blowing about the lawn by then, and if one of these came within the hen's visual field she immediately raised her head to glance at it and was off in a flash. I wanted to repeat all this with different coloured tapes and trying them coronal in direction as well as sagittal, but I shall have to wait for a grant from the Medical Research Council.


## Oh, the doing and undoing

I don't know whether it's worth reading the medical journals each week (except of course for this column). My brain gets very battered having new facts put in so often and then having them extracted again. I was thinking last night of the number of things I have read which I later find refuted in another article, sometimes within a few months: just when I'd mugged up about fibrinoid necrosis of glomeruli

4

causing vicious circle hypertension, I read elsewhere that all rats have got fibrinoid necrosis anyway and that the other work might be invalid. Just when I had it clear that crush syndrome kidneys got cortical necrosis from a nervous mechanism making the medullary bypass open out and the cortical vessels close down, somebody says that the cortical vessels are squashed by swollen cells and it isn't a nervous mechanism at all. Again, what about breast milk? I've read in the last year that thyroid increased it, then that iodine alone was better still, and just lately that iodine doesn't increase it after all.

I really don't know what to believe or which side to take. If one keeps on packing and unpacking a suitcase with different contents everything gets muddled, containers burst, and toothpowder and hair lotion impregnate the shirts and socks. That's what's going to happen to our brains if we go on poking in facts and plucking them out at the same time.

Some beliefs are cherished a long time before some pundit kills them for us, and the extraction of a firm rooted belief is as unpleasant as the removal of an impacted wisdom tooth. I was brought up to believe that pulmonary oedema was due to left ventricular failure, but apparently it isn't today. As a student I fondly believed digitalis worked by shielding the ventricles from the futile rampagings of the auricles above them, but the Hammersmith chaps say I must cross it all out now and talk about right auricular pressure. We used to be taught that the rock dust and not the coal dust hurt the miners' lungs, but I see that the coal dust is the villain after all. Spina bifida has nothing whatever to do with enuresis, though it had when I was a boy. Though I'm anything but clever, as Captain Corcoran remarked, I could talk like this for ever.

What's to be done? I'm getting suspicious and distrustful of all medical literature, and I've a jolly good mind to cancel my subscription to the *Lancet* and become a stockbroker. Stocks and shares are no more variable than medical theory, and one can make money out of *their* fluctuations.

## Light, or sticky, fingers

I'm curious to know if there is as much theft at other hospitals as at mine. I hide in the anonymity of this column because if my own hospital is the only one where everyone steals I don't want to expose it.

What gets stolen? Well, nearly everything. If new blankets are issued to the wards they go; if large towels are supplied to the theatres for the surgeons they stay only a few days; lavatory paper is removed as often as it is supplied. Because of this patients are colder, surgeons are damper, and everyone is constipated. The whole standard of hospital comfort could be much higher if only people would be reasonably honest.

I was talking to the head gardener this morning and he told me that he always allows for 20% loss when setting out plants; the other day 19 geranium plants were stolen in an hour while the man planting them went to lunch. We thought it would be a kind act to supply books and magazines for our outpatients and we expected a few to go, but we didn't expect every single one to go on the very first day – which was what happened.

The dishonesty doesn't seem to be confined to any one class. In the hospital library, which only the doctors use, books and periodicals disappear with alarming speed. When I was staying the other week at a well known Oxford hotel, full of respectable prosperous people, the waiter told me that since the war all their silver teaspoons and silver tankards had gone and that many guests left with bath mats, rugs, ash trays, and table napkins.

I don't want to sound like a testy old gentleman writing to *The Times*, but I do think standards of honesty are getting lower everywhere. I know it's partly because so many goods are scarce, but I'm afraid that when everything is more plentiful the dishonesty habit will have come to stay.

## Three types of unambiguity

There's been a lot of talk lately about choosing people suitable for various careers, especially for medicine. Everyone agrees that intelligence tests alone are not enough. I believe the following additional quotients are necessary, and I await suggestions how to measure them. Taken together with the intelligence quotient they would give a very fair measurement of personality.

The *Bee in Bonnet Quotient* (BIBQ) assesses the prejudice coefficient of a man. A doctor with a high BIBQ will hold one belief to the exclusion of all others and will find some diagnosis in his particular specialty to fit every complaint. Nevertheless, his constancy of purpose and unflagging application may bring him success where others have failed. Research workers should have low BIBQs, or they will discover only what they believe. Reformers should have high BIBQs, lest they get bored with repetition or dismayed by repeated failure. The bee in bonnet type of man is liable to be tedious and unpopular in community life, but he is useful because he gets things done.

The *Goat Getting Quotient* (GGQ) is highly important, for it measures the degree to which the candidate gets other people's goats. It depends on thick skinnedness, lack of tact, the possession of irritating personal habits, and so on. Intelligent people surprisingly often have a high GGQ, and less able people may be preferable for a post because others can work with them. It isn't always easy to see how these

7

remarkable goat getting properties arise, but everyone knows the type that though free from major defects manages to rub others up the wrong way.

Then there is the *Goose Booing Quotient* (GBQ), expressing ability to say boo to a goose. This is the inverse of the *Yes Man Coefficient*, which can be expressed as YMC. A high GBQ is an asset to the intelligent but a menace in the hands of a fool, for to have the courage of one's convictions is useless if the convictions are foolish, and leads to senseless aggression. A high GBQ is essential for iconoclasts, deans of medical schools, and chairmen of committees. Those with low GBQs are a delight to dictatorial medical superintendents or fierce ward sisters, who find them a pleasure to handle; they also make good housemen for chiefs who make mistakes but do not wish to be corrected.

So there are four headings under which you can jot down impressions of your fellow men: intelligence, bee in bonnet, goat getting, and goose booing. We already have matrix tests, etc, for intelligence; no doubt psychologists will evolve appropriate methods for measuring the others.

## Give us another one, do

When I first had an article published the part I most enjoyed was ordering reprints and proudly posting them to all my friends to show them I really had got something in the *Lancet*. That was early in the war, when I was paid about a fifth of my present salary and was at least five times richer. Now I have had a few more articles published I am getting less enthusiastic about the reprint business. Whatever the article one gets quite a lot of requests for reprints, and when they cost as much as two shillings each it is no joke giving them free to large numbers of strange doctors (mostly in America) who have dispatched printed cards asking for them, or to secretaries of American libraries who have done the same.

To reduce excessive traffic in reprints, any doctor who is sufficiently interested in a medical paper to want one ought to make the effort to write a personal note – it's better manners, it's more amusing for the author, and it allows a word or two of comment or criticism which may be instructive (American papers please copy). Admittedly some of the printed forms are models of politeness and praise:

> We would be greatly appreciative of receiving two copies of your most interesting article entitled "Struve's Terrible Unilateral Anaemia" published in the *Lancet*, Vol *i*, No *6234*, Date *Feb 20*, Year *1943*, Page *249*, and any other reprints of a similar nature.

But of what value is the sterile flattery of the printed word? I am sure that if the habit spreads (and it is now common in England) we shall soon find little cards for sale at bookstalls thus:

Parent
Dear Sibling. Thank you so much for the delightful Friend
Christmas
*bedsocks* which you gave me for my birthday.
my wedding present
They are most *comforting*. Thank you again. I should greatly appreciate any other gifts of a similar nature.
Affectionately,
Yours Sincerely, *Arthur*.
Ever,

I am not going to sign this communication because (*a*) you might think I was showing off that I had had several articles printed; (*b*) you might think I was trying to get a refund of two shillings a copy from America; or (*c*) you might write and ask me for a reprint.

## *Buzz, buzz*

In the Barnes Hall of the Royal Society of Medicine the bell push which rings to the lantern operator has been ingeniously placed at the point on the lecturer's desk where his right elbow naturally presses if he leans on the desk. I have been making a study of the reaction of different lecturers as they lean on this push button. I should like to read a paper on this subject at the Royal Society of Medicine, but as I am nervous of leaning on it myself I have decided to publish my results in this column.

Firstly, there is the very nervous man. He starts off safely enough standing well behind the desk. The cruel thing is that the buzzer doesn't catch him till his first moment of confidence; then, when he is just warming up, he leans confidently forwards on the desk and immediately reverberating buzzing fills the entire hall. His talk falters and stops. He gazes round with a wild surmise, wondering if it is a firebell or whether it is a special alarm to show that he has spoken too long. He is far too nervous to realise he is ringing it himself. He leans there wretchedly, his elbow still on the bell, and tries to speak through the noise. Various members of the audience try to signal to him that he is leaning on the bell push, but in his nervous state he cannot comprehend them and begins vaguely to wonder what is wrong with him. Are his trousers coming down? Has he said something rude by mistake? At last, the secretary of the meeting leans sideways from his seat on the dais and tells him what he is doing; with a muttered apology he lifts his elbow and the buzzing noise stops. Then he starts again in dead silence, but he is a broken man, his confidence shattered, his flow of words less coherent; for the rest of the talk he eyes the bell push like an unexploded bomb.

Then, the moderately nervous man. He reacts somewhat differently because, though nervous, he is sufficiently orientated to realise what has happened. As soon as the buzzer rings he shies like a startled horse and his elbow jerks off the button as if he had got an electric shock.

The dishonest man pretends he meant to ring the bell on purpose and firmly says, "I rang the bell for the first slide please," even though he had no intention of showing it yet. It is remarkable that the lantern operator, invisible in his wooden tower, can after years of experience always tell whether a push on the button is inadvertent or advertent so to speak, but he may be defeated by the dishonest lecturer.

The really confident extrovert deals with the buzzer in quite a different way. When the shattering noise first starts he beams at his audience and says, "I believe I'm leaning on the buzzer," then he shouts across the room to the operator, "I don't want a slide yet, I'm leaning on the buzzer." Then leisurely he lifts his elbow and resumes his talk. Men of such powerful calibre are rare and few speakers can survive the ordeal by buzz without severe psychic trauma. Selye's work on the adaptation reaction shows what irreparable harm can be produced by alarm and stress. Eosinophil counts before and after leaning on the bell push might be revealing.

Maybe some responsible person will read this and move the bell to a safer position; but perhaps it would be a shame to remove this hazard, which has for so many years entertained the audience during the less exciting lectures.

# II

## *Apriority*

Published in the *Lancet* 23 December 1961

One of the most important things about treatment is that it should *be* effective – not merely that it *ought* to be effective. A remedy which is known to work, though nobody knows why, is preferable to a remedy which has the support of theory without the confirmation of practice.

J W Todd emphasises this, both in his book[1] and in his article on the history of medicine.[2] He applies the words *a priori* to the reasoning behind many traditional treatments. For my part I agree with Gowers[3] that writers could probably get along quite well without *a priori*, and I dislike the expression for I never can remember exactly what it means. I think my difficulty is partly due to its having several subdivisions of meaning.

There is little doubt about its general sense. It describes the arguments, reasoning, speculations, notions, traditions, or other support for conclusions which have not been backed by any kind of practical experiment. When I think of the *a priori* grounds for many of the futile treatments that used to

---

[1] Todd J W, ed. *Text book of clinical medicine*. London: Pitman Medical, 1960.
[2] Todd J W. *Lancet* 1961; ii: 480.
[3] Gowers E P. *Complete plain words*. London: HM Stationery Office, 1954.

be given and still are given, I realise what many fine shades of apriority[1] there are. I set them out now.


*Shades of meaning*

(1) There are some things we are so sure of that we accept them without proof. They are assumptions which we act on without question, and they cannot be proved. The Kantian school of philosophy applied the term *a priori* to reasoning based on such things. They held that such ideas – for example, that good health is more to be desired than bad, or that doctors should prefer effective treatment to ineffective – are inborn, inherent within the mind, and independent of experience. I prefer to say that they are damned obvious. Todd suggests that *a priori* argument is always worthless, but this kind is not. We could not get anywhere without these unprovable assumptions.

(2) The witchcraft type of treatment – "eye of newt and toe of frog, wool of bat and tongue of dog" – of which many examples still exist, is based on no reasoning whatever. It is just a wild senseless concoction, with not even an assumed axiom to back it. An example in modern times is the use of a brown mess of powdered fossilised fish mixed with glycerin to spread on erysipelas (glycerin of icthyol is still applied today, although backed by sulphonamides). This sort of nonsense has nothing behind it except sheer imagination, the desire to concoct an elaborate and disgusting potion, and a trace of the two primitive ideas: (*a*) anything unpleasant is good for you (the inverted Marie Lloyd theme – that is, "a little of what you don't fancy does you good"); and (*b*) anything difficult to get, rare, or expensive

---

[1] Synthesised by Asher in the Etymologico-Semantic Laboratories, London (patent pending).

is more likely to be effective than something cheap, common, and easily got.[1] Todd would call the basis of such mumbojumbo *a priori*, but there hardly seems enough assumption behind it to justify it. Nomenclature is difficult, but perhaps "pure unadulterated boloney" might do (PUB).

(3) Gradually moving up the scale (grading *a priori* treatments according to their boloney content, with the boloney content diminishing as we advance), we come to the higher forms of witchcraft, which are backed by theories which, though patently nonsensical, do contain minute traces of theoretical reasoning. Though the administration of bats' blood for insomnia is pure boloney, I maintain that treating insomnia with the blood of dormice (as has been repeatedly advocated by Asher)[2] is not wholly devoid of reason. Nor for that matter is the practice of fumigating and scrubbing an operating theatre after a death, rightly condemned by Forbes[3]; because such things, though unsupported by experience, are at least backed by reasoning of a kind – that is, that there is something in the blood of dormice which promotes sleep and that the spirit of a patient who has died in the theatre will linger on and be a general nuisance unless exorcised. This sort of nonsense might be called HBC (high boloney content) as opposed to PUB, the pure variety described above. Moreover, something which was PUB

---

[1] Field Marshall Naaman, who had leprosy, heard of a very good skin man through his wife's maid. He went to see him, with encouragement from the King, and arrived in the equivalent of a Bentley, prepared to pay a large fee for the invocations and laying on of hands which he expected. He was bitterly incensed when he got a simple prescription for river water and was charged nothing. "Sir," his servants pointed out, "if the prophet had asked you to do elaborate things you'd have done them, wouldn't you? Why not try the simple thing?" (Adapted from *II Kings*, V, 1-14.)

[2] Asher R A J. *Middlesex Hosp J* 1960; February: 9.

[3] Forbes R. *Lancet* 1946; ii: 293.

when first advocated by some wild witch may reach HBC status later because it acquires the backing of a reasonable assumption – that is, "treatment which is alleged to do good is more likely to be helpful than treatment which has never been advocated by anyone." There is obviously some sense in that, although it is an argument that has perpetuated more harmful or useless procedures than any other.

(4) Going one grade higher still, we come to forms of treatment which, though not supported by scientific experiment, have a fairly reasonable theoretical basis. I will term this PCB (pretty convincing boloney). I am thinking of ideas such as: that rough or "strong" food will provoke a stomach afflicted by ulcer; that a man whose temperature falls below normal because of shock should be heated up till it becomes normal; and many other such things. Here the arguments are, though *a priori*, of a far more civilised standard that the "eye of newt" variety. Their use by medical men arises from the unsound practice of acting on theoretical grounds without bothering to determine whether experience confirms the theoretical benefits; yet PCB differs from the next grade because if more care had been spent on the theory a more effective conclusion might have been reached. For instance, there are *a priori* reasons for *not* heating a shocked person, if you assume that the vital organs benefit from the blood lent to them from the cold and bloodless skin.

(5) The most reasonable and forgivable kind of *a priori* treatment is the one where you give a remedy which theoretically ought to work, even though properly controlled clinical trials have not yet been conducted to make sure that it does.

I refer here to treatments based on scientific experiments. For example, if the bacteria grown from a patient are killed *in vitro* by one antibiotic and not by another, it is plain that the former should be given rather than the latter.

I am not sure whether this could be called an *a priori* argument, since the exact limits of the term depend on who uses it. One dictionary definition of *a priori* gives "theoretical" as one of its meanings,[1] and the treatment of infections with antibiotics to which they are sensitive in the laboratory is certainly theoretical. Moreover, we all see organisms which are highly sensitive in laboratory tests fail to disappear when the appropriate antibiotic is given; whereas organisms which appear virtually immortal when tested on an agar plate may quickly expire *in vivo* when exposed to an antibiotic which is theoretically ineffective.

One can call this type of treatment *a priori* because it is theoretical (and not always practical); but if the term is restricted to arguments based on assumed axioms – that is, *pure* armchair reasoning – then treatment which is supported by scientific *experiments* does not qualify as *a priori*.

Whether we use the word or not, it is certainly true that many things which in theory ought to be highly effective turn out in practice to be completely useless. We could call this type of treatment UBC, or uncertain boloney content.

*Conclusion*

The best way to decide which remedies are good is "try them and see." The question to which we must always find an answer is not "should it work?" but "does it work?" (even if we do not know why).

*Summary*

*Experientia docet.*

[1] *Shorter Oxford dictionary*. London, 1956.

# III

## *For to admire*

Extract from an obituary of Frederick Parkes Weber, published in the *Lancet* 16 June 1962

I feel as if I had known Parkes Weber a long time, but I never met him till the last fifth of his life. To me he was always a remarkable old man. I cannot visualise him as a remarkable young man, though I know that once he must have been so. His name was a legend to me long before I ever met him. I had heard the story of the time he stood up in the Royal Society of Medicine and said: "I have never heard of Turner's Syndrome," and how there was a stamping of feet and cheering for a long time, because it was unthinkable that there could be a syndrome of which Parkes Weber had not heard.

When he came to see a case in consultation he would write down everything in longhand, going into great detail. All the dates must be correct. The doctor's name must be spelt right. He would take a long and careful history with patient, unhurried thoroughness. He wrote it all down, slowly and carefully. I always allowed plenty of time if he was going to see a patient, and I never grudged it to him. The earnest detailed inquiries, the painstaking elaborate notes, the minutes ticking by, and lunch long past. He was so interested in the patient all other things were forgotten. He filed all these notes with great care, building up a unique record of all the rarities he had seen and often referring to them again and following up the patient's progress. "Five years ago, you asked me to see a patient called . . . with . . . . I wonder if you have seen her recently and if you can let me know. . . ." When he finished a consultation he had not finished with the patient; he would go on collecting more facts as long as the patient lived.

He wore the kind of glasses that professors ought to wear. He looked like a professor. He was a professor. He behaved like a professor; he lost all contact with the world when he was immersed in thought. One of my happiest memories of him was the night he came to dinner with me. I wanted someone worthy of his conversation and so I asked a friend who is curator of medieval manuscripts at the British Museum. They were soon engaged in deep discussion on the exact wording of a fourteenth century manuscript. The subtleties of their argument were beyond me, but I got enormous pleasure listening to these two experts talking about things I did not understand. They waved spoons at each other to emphasise points, and they ate anything near to them in an abstracted way. Parkes Weber ate most of my roll of bread by mistake and then tried to eat a cheese straw with a pudding spoon; he was in the fourteenth century. When they left they were still in deep conversation about another manuscript; somehow, as they drifted towards the front door quoting little bits of Latin, they both managed to get into the bathroom together, still locked in learned controversy.

You might think that because he was an expert on diseases which were rare and usually untreatable he was the kind of doctor more concerned with diseases than with patients. You would be wrong. He was beloved by his patients. He had old-fashioned and very beautiful manners. He treated patients with grave courtesy and listened intently to everything they had to say. After consulting with the doctor he always went back to the patient and said something kind and encouraging. He shook them earnestly by the hand and said goodbye in a way that made them feel he was really sorry to go. He was loved not only by patients but by everybody who came into contact with him. He had great charm. His face was always radiant with interest and good will. He liked everybody and was interested in everything.

# IV

## The physical basis
## of mental illness

Published in the *Medical Society's Transactions*, Vol LXX, 1953-4

There are two ways of considering the physical basis of mental illness. Firstly, to discuss those physical diseases which can cause mental illness; secondly, to examine the possibility of there being physical causes for the other primary psychoses – schizophrenia, maniac depressive insanity, and so on. I am going to confine myself mainly to the first approach.

As well as my general medical wards at the Central Middlesex Hospital I have a mental observation ward, through which pass about 700 patients a year. So in the last 10 years I have seen around 7000 mental observation cases. Being a physician and not a psychiatrist I have tried to filter off those cases where there seemed a chance of finding an organic cause for the mental illness. The primary psychoses have been transferred to mental hospitals.

The proportion of cases where relevant organic disease is found is probably under 10%, but detecting these cases is satisfying to the clinician, and treatment is often rewarding. In trying to detect organic cases I have found that the mental symptoms were not of great help, except that visual hallucinations are rather suggestive of toxic causes and that grandiose delusions (though far from invariable) are common in general paralysis of the insane. The essentials in seeking the organic case are a full history of the symptoms and a complete physical examination. The very simple observations, such as whether the patient looks ill, whether he has a temperature, or whether he looks wasted, are often the factors that first reveal an organic cause.

Some organic causes of mental symptoms

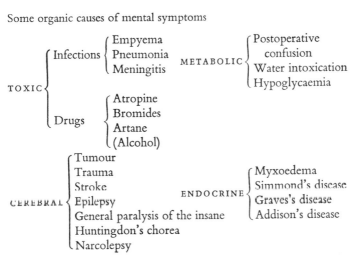

The table shows a rough classification of some of the organic causes for mental confusion that have turned up in the mental observation wards. I have confined the list to conditions I have actually met – for instance, I have not put down mercury among the toxic causes, although it can cause a severe psychosis, because I have never met a case.

## Infections

An old lady of 78 with no previous mental illness but a story of pneumonia two months previously was admitted with three weeks' confusion and restlessness. She had wandered round the house believing that black men were coming in through the windows trying to knife her and believing her neighbours were plotting against her. Routine examination of the chest indicated fluid at the left base, and aspiration removed a pint of pneumococcal pus, although she had no rise of temperature. With intercostal drainage and penicillin injected into the empyema cavity her mental symptoms disappeared in a week and her empyema cleared in a fortnight. Followed up for two years there was no further mental trouble or chest illness.

A milkman of 30 was brought in by the police after two days' violent behaviour at home, where he had attacked his family and thrown furniture at the windows. When I first saw him he was stark naked, running round and round the padded room calling out "Milk O'." His neck was held in a rigid full extension and a fine purpuric rash covered his body. His violence was so great that penthothal was required before lumbar puncture, which produced the ginger beer turbidity of meningococcal meningitis. With sulphadiazine treatment he made a rapid recovery from his meningitis and his confusion.

A carpenter of 25 was referred by his practitioner to the relieving officer for admission as a mental case because he had been accusing his relatives of poisoning him and complaining of terrifying faces floating all round him. The relieving officer said as he brought him in: "He's breathing very fast doctor, and he has little blisters on his lips, I wondered if he had pneumonia." He was perfectly correct; there was extensive consolidation of the right upper lobe. The appropriate treatment for his pneumonia resulted in rapid improvement.

I have mentioned three examples to show that infections can be mistaken for mental cases – empyema, pneumonia, and meningococcal meningitis. I have seen many similar cases. A mistake by the practitioner is most understandable when mental symptoms are so prominent and also because violent behaviour may make physical examination in the home almost impossible. Among other infections, I have seen general peritonitis from a perforated appendicitis in the puerperium admitted as a case of puerperal psychosis.

*Drugs*

There are numerous drugs that can cause a toxic psychosis. Among those I have encountered are atropine, bromides, and artane. As regards atropine, it was remarked by John Gerarde in 1597 in his famous Herball that "belladonna bringeth madnesse if a few of the berries be inwardly taken." Atropine administered regularly as eyedrops or in a mixture for Parkinson's disease or asthma can cause gross confusion and disorientation with hallucinosis that can easily be mistaken for a senile psychosis if the dry mouth and large pupils are not observed. I saw one lady with a psychosis from atropine eye drops admitted on two occasions as an eye hospital put her back on the drops again a year after her first attack. Bromism is more common, and I have had six cases admitted under the Lunacy Act. In a case of psychosis in a previously normal elderly hypertensive patient it is well worth taking the blood bromide, particularly if there are visual hallucinations. Above 200 mg/100 ml mental symptoms are common; above 300 mg/100 ml they are almost invariable. Stopping the bromides and giving 2 g of sodium chloride thrice daily quickly restores mental balance. It is particularly important to spot bromism as otherwise elderly patients may continue on bromides to quieten their mental symptoms when all the time they are causing them. In cases of Parkinson's disease with psychosis it is worth finding out what antitremulants are being taken. One old lady I saw last year admitted with an artane psychosis recovered with abstinence, but persuaded me to try small doses again because she said it was the only thing that helped her parkinsonism. She became completely disorientated and confused again within three days but recovered once more when the drug was stopped.

The oddest drug psychosis I have seen was from ephedrine. A young science student, an asthmatic, found ephedrine stimulated him and kept him awake, so he got into the habit of taking up to 20 half grain tablets in the evening. After a particularly large dose he was admitted as an acute schizophrenic psychosis. He recovered in three days and told me what he had been taking. My ward sister tells me that her small son aged 8 becomes hallucinated after two quarter grain ephedrine tablets and sees trains moving on the ceiling.

Alcohol is not often prescribed as a drug, but it can be conveniently included here. Its manifestations of course include acute alcoholic confusion (that is ordinary drunk and disorderly); delirium tremens, with its vivid and terrifying visual hallucinations; and Korsakov's psychosis, in which a patient will give in a rational and convincing manner an entirely fictitious but often credible account of an imaginary experience. Delirium tremens and Korsakov's psychosis, if not typical, can mimic other psychoses and be quite difficult to diagnose, especially in the secret drinker.

While discussing toxic psychoses I must tell you about a patient I saw this afternoon in my outpatient clinic. An iron moulder of 40 arrived and told me that for three months a strange smell was emanating from his body and his breath – so strong that his friends and relations were shunning him – and caused by a poisonous gas having entered his body while at work.

You will agree that this kind of story is highly suggestive of delusional insanity, and had there not been a very helpful letter from the man's practitioner I would certainly have doubted his sanity. I learned from this letter that the man had been working with tellurium and that a peculiar chemical garlic like smell is a well known symptom of tellurium ingestion and may persist for many months after exposure. (The odour is due to the excretion of dimethyltelluride.) Further confirmation of the truth of this was soon obtained when an intense garlic like smell began to fill the consulting room to the discomfiture of myself and the students. This was not, of course, a toxic psychosis but a toxic condition imitating a psychosis; all the same I thought it could fairly be included here.

*Cerebral causes*

I remember vividly a doctor's daughter aged 30 sent to the psychiatric outpatient clinic for admission to mental hospital as a case of hebephrenic schizophrenia. For six months she had been increasingly apathetic and listless, she was forgetful, slovenly, and occasionally incontinent of urine and faeces. Examination showed considerable papilloedema and slight nystagmus. At craniotomy a cerebellar cyst was removed and she became a bright and normal person within a week.

A woman department supervisor in a factory was superintending the orderly descent of the girls under her charge into an air raid shelter when a flying bomb fell. A clock above her head dropped on her; she received no other injury. She was unconscious for half an hour. On becoming conscious again she behaved so violently and irrationally that she had to be admitted to the mental observation ward. Though normally an unusually responsible and capable person, she behaved in the ward in almost an uncontrollable fashion, biting and scratching those around her and deliberately dirtying her bed. She denied that she lived in

Willesden, or that she had ever worked in a factory, and refused to believe that there was a war on. She remained in this state for two months, and just when it was thought this traumatic psychosis was going to be permanent she started gradually to recover her memory and her behaviour, and within a fortnight she had become her normal and charming self. She has remained perfectly well since, and it seemed impossible to believe the polite and able supervisor and the obscene she devil were the same person, and that one blow could produce such a change.

Strokes are fairly common as a cause of a sudden psychotic change in an old person. The stroke may be very mild in its physical effects (for instance, producing only weakness and clumsiness of one hand and slight speech difficulty) and yet be accompanied by severe mental disturbance for several days. Another way stroke can produce an apparent psychosis is when there is jargon aphasia from involvement of the speech centre. The extraordinary stream of nonsense that issues from the lips of these people can at first be mistaken for sheer mental confusion, and only when the clinician asks the patient to name a few familiar objects does the neurological lesion become apparent. Subarachnoid haemorrhage can rarely present as a psychosis. I have seen two cases. One of them was a young clerk of 25, who went to the lavatory a normal, sane person and emerged five minutes later violent, disorientated, and completely irrational. Because he had neck rigidity on routine examination a lumbar puncture was done, which showed deeply blood stained fluid; he had not complained of headache presumably because of the gross mental disturbance. Probably this patient had ruptured his berry aneurysm while straining at stool.

As well as producing in long standing cases a chronic aggressive personality change, a single epileptic fit can be followed by a temporary acute psychosis lasting a few days.

The severity of the individual fit seems quite unrelated to the severity of the psychosis, and during the psychotic stage the patient may show behaviour exactly like that of schizophrenia or hysteria, and yet after a few days become surprisingly normal.

General paralysis of the insane is an important condition to diagnose early, for the sooner the treatment the better the prognosis. Its manifestations are protean, and less than half the cases show the classic delusions of grandeur; the others present with simple dementia, endogenous depression, outbursts of sudden violence, or almost any psychotic change. Physical signs may be scanty, and it is one of the conditions where laboratory investigation is much more reliable than clinical examination; the paretic Lange and positive Wassermann reaction and other cerebrospinal fluid changes are remarkably constant. I have found that the face is often helpful in suggesting the diagnosis – the combination of vacuousness, fatuousness, and ptosis gives a look of benevolent fatuity that can be almost diagnostic.

Among cerebral causes for psychosis I have put in Huntington's chorea. This is not so rare, about 15 cases in 10 years. The onset between 40 and 50, the family history, the bizarre continuous movements, and the inevitable downhill progress make diagnosis fairly easy, useless though it is.

Lastly, I have included narcolepsy, although I have had only three cases of my own, of which only one presented as a psychosis. Before I describe the patient may I remind you of the features of this rather recherche condition. There are four components of it: (a) paroxysmal attacks of sleep (narcolepsy); (b) attacks of weakness amounting almost to paralysis during emotion (cataplexy); (c) vivid hallucinations, especially on going off to sleep (hypnagogic hallucinosis); (d) sudden paralysis while going off to sleep (sleep paralysis).

A man of 59 was admitted to the observation ward in February 1951 with one month's visual hallucinations and a story of having collapsed after a quarrel with his daughter. He recovered in a few days and was discharged after a fortnight, diagnosed as doubtful bromidism. (He had been taking small doses of bromide and had a slightly raised blood level.) Two months later he was readmitted to the mental observation ward with the hallucinations worse than ever; he complained of seeing the faces of friends who had died floating round him and black things crawling over the bed. He said the hallucinations were very vivid and bothered him only while going off to sleep. I had quite missed the diagnosis on his first admission, but this time his description of the hallucinations was so striking that the diagnosis occurred to me, and once the appropriate questions were asked it became obvious. Firstly, he admitted to several years' attacks of drowsiness in which he had to rush for a chair or couch before he fell asleep. Secondly, he said if he met someone unexpectedly he had such trembling and weakness he had to flop down in a chair. Also, in the first admission he had mentioned "collapsing with rage" after a quarrel with his daughter. Thirdly, he said he had been having bouts of these hallucinations for several years, always when going off to sleep and always strikingly vivid, and lastly he had often, while going to sleep, had a peculiar feeling of generalised tingling in which he found himself utterly unable to move till he managed to jerk one limb, when full power would return. As with other cases of narcolepsy the response to amphetamine was dramatic, and on methedrine 5 mg three times daily his hallucinations stopped, as did his narcolepsy, cataplexy, and sleep paralysis. He was followed in outpatients for the next nine months and said he was a different person, free of hallucinations and other symptoms and 100% better than before.

Among the metabolic disturbances all surgeons have seen mental confusion after extensive operations, presumably due to some alteration in blood chemistry, and we sometimes see after severe diarrhoea a confusional state due to salt loss from the bowel being inadequately replaced in the water intake and causing a low blood sodium and so called water intoxication.

As regards hypoglycaemia, probably all of us have our favourite hypoglycaemic stories because the mental symptoms are so remarkable and so varied. I know one diabetic who when he was hypoglycaemic started eating the flowers in the vase by his bed. Another man, a most respectable chemist, used to rush into the adjacent female ward as soon as his blood sugar fell and make unwelcome advances to the women there. A diabetic houseman I once had, used during a round to become abnormally polite and start saying "Excuse me sir, I beg your pardon sir," until I could persuade him to eat some sugar. I have had only two hypoglycaemic people admitted as mental cases: one was brought in from the street and one was transferred from a surgical ward, both with insulin overdosage. To have a maniacal patient careering round the padded cell drenched with sweat, to give him two syringefuls of 50% glucose and watch his miraculous return to sanity in front of a gallery of students, is a dramatic pleasure too rarely accorded to the physician. Islet cell tumours can of course give a similar picture, and the three cases I have seen in the wards of my colleagues had all long histories of psychotic and psychoneurotic behaviour due to spontaneous hypoglycaemia. I have not had the luck to encounter a case of islet tumour admitted to my observation ward as a mental case, but I may have missed several. Difficulty in wakening the patient in the morning and psychotic behaviour before breakfast seem constant and helpful clues to the detection of these rare but satisfying cases.

## Endocrine disorders

I have seen both thyrotoxic crisis and addisonian crisis associated with psychotic symptoms, but there is not time to describe these. I will confine myself to myxoedema and Simmond's disease. Myxoedema as a cause of psychosis is, I think, important because it is by no means rare (20 cases having been admitted to the mental observation ward in the last 10 years) and the recovery of the mental symptoms with thyroid treatment is usually dramatic. An excellent description of the condition was given in 1888 by a special committee of the Clinical Society of London, who said: "Insanity as a complication of myxoedema is noted in nearly half the cases" (in those days, of course, there was no treatment). It takes the form of acute or chronic mania, dementia, or melancholia, with a marked predominance of suspicion and self accusation. A J Cronin in his novel *The Citadel* described a case, though in less sober language. The hero, a struggling young doctor, being called to certify a dangerous lunatic noticed the unusual appearance of the face and non-pitting oedema of the body and, to quote from the novel: "Suddenly something vibrated like an electric terminal in his brain. He had it, by God, he had it. It was myxoedema." I will describe only a few of the 20 cases we have had.

Mrs R was admitted on a three day order with a year's peculiar behaviour alternating between excitement and depression. She was depressed, confused, and persecuted, accusing her husband of poisoning her and believing others were plotting to harm her. When anyone approached her bed she clung to them begging for mercy and muttered incoherent nonsense about fire and water and vengeance.

Her appearance showed advanced myxoedema: her face was bloated, there was a butterfly shaped burgundy flush on her cheeks and nose, the skin was rough, cold, and thick. Her voice was low and husky, her lips were thickened. The pulse was 60 beats/minute, the blood cholesterol raised (364 mg/100 ml). The basal metabolic rate was impossible to take. A history from her relatives gave the typical story of gaining weight, sensitivity to cold, deafness, alteration of facial appearance, loss of hair, and so on. The change in her appearance after two months' thyroid treatment was very striking. Her psychotic symptoms cleared up completely after five weeks on thyroid, and she has continued to attend outpatients for the last seven years well in all ways.

Mrs S was admitted on a three day order, referred by the psychiatric department of another hospital as a case of paranoid psychosis. For three months she had complained that people were spying on her down ventilator pipes, and she was hearing voices saying unpleasant things about her at night. She also gave a story of two years' dry skin, falling hair, and deepening voice, and said she felt so cold and sleepy she wanted to curl up and go into a long, long sleep. After a fortnight's treatment with thyroid her appearance had improved and she had some insight into her hallucinations, realising that they were not real voices even though she still heard them; after three weeks her blood cholesterol had come down from 250 to 120 mg/100 ml, the hallucinations had stopped, and she said: "I feel different, I see things different, and my husband says I look younger. I talk different. I've lost that deep tone, and speak lighter." She has remained well mentally and physically and four years later continues to attend my endocrine outpatients.

I have found photographic records before and after treatment most helpful in confirming the diagnosis, as accurate basal metabolic rates are usually impossible in psychotic cases and even in sane cases are far from infallible.

Myxoedema is not an easy disease to diagnose except in the gross case, and it is a pity that textbooks usually illustrate myxoedema only with gross cases and rarely include milder examples, because the less flagrant cases can have severe symptoms. The voice and the appearance are usually the features that suggest the diagnosis, but may I also add that very loud snoring is common and that the position in bed may be helpful – one might almost call it the snug sign.

Lastly, a case of Simmond's disease. Mrs A was first admitted to the mental observation ward in 1948 suffering from mental confusion and hallucinations. There was a history of her being "peculiar" for many years, staying in bed almost all day, taking no interest in the outside world, and having occasional bouts of stupor lasting one or two days. I made a note that she looked ill and rather pale and that she had delusions of persecution and visual hallucinations. I never thought of the diagnosis, but labelled her as some kind of organic dementia. She was certified and transferred to a mental hospital, where she remained for six months with no improvement, but finally was taken home by her relatives.

A year later she was readmitted to my mental observation ward with the same story. On this second occasion her somewhat prematurely aged appearance, her pallor, and her pseudomyxoedematous appearance struck me, and to quote Cronin: "Suddenly something vibrated like an electrical terminal in my brain. I had it by God, I had it. It was Simmond's." Once thought of the diagnosis was obvious, and I much regretted not having thought of it before. All her symptoms dated from the birth of her second child 20 years ago. The labour had been followed by severe bleeding due to retained placenta, and afterwards most of her hair fell out. Ever since then she had never menstruated at all, never lactated, she had been apathetic and listless with bouts of coma. She felt abnormally cold all the time and was always drowsy. For 20 years she had given up attempting to do any housework and for three years had been in bed all day. Physical examination showed complete absence of pubic and axillary hair, absence of breast tissue, and atrophy of the vagina and uterus. The skin was dry, the temperature subnormal, and the pulse slow. The history and examination were really enough to be certain, but for completeness the two relevant tests were done: (*a*) ketosteroids were almost completely absent from the urine; (*b*) she showed hypoglycaemic unresponsiveness – that is to say her blood sugar did not return to its previous level one and a half hours after giving five units of insulin. With testosterone treatment the physical improvement was remarkable. The pubic hair grew again, the breasts developed, and the morale developed strikingly. After 20 years' virtual hibernation this woman was within six months walking unsupported and beginning to take up the reins of her household, which she had relinquished 20 years ago. It is very tempting to say she became mentally quite normal, but that would not be true. She became enormously improved in her sanity, lost her delusions completely, and was free of hallucinations for over a year, returning to her home and house duties; but she continued thereafter to have periods of visual hallucinosis, and in one of these she was admitted to mental hospital and died suddenly. Autopsy confirmed the diagnosis – the pituitary gland being almost completely atrophied. In a way it is not surprising that 20 years' complete endocrine starvation had left some irreversible damage to her mind.

That completes the examples of physical causes for mental illness that I am describing. I have left out many: for instance, psychoses secondary to encephalitis lethargica, those secondary to blindness and deafness, and those occurring in the puerperium. I have left out the senile psychoses because I am uncertain whether there is adequate evidence of any organic lesions. Cerebral atherosclerosis is common in the brains of senile psychotics, but is there controlled evidence to show it is more common than in the brains of sane people of the same age?

Lastly, it is hard to resist touching on the possibility of there being physical causes for other mental illnesses – those we label mania, melancholia, schizophrenia, and so on. One difficulty is that at present there is no sign, no symptom, no pathological test which can confirm the diagnosis of a primary psychosis beyond question. Mental diseases do not fall comfortably into the compartments classified for them. One sees cases that have some features of schizophrenia and some of mania; others that fluctuate from one psychotic diagnosis to another.

In trying to diagnose these cases correctly are we forcing them into compartments that should not be there? Are we drawing arbitrary divisions in what is really a continuous spectrum. Do these different diseases really exist as noso-logical entities or are they artificial distinctions made to comfort ourselves with the illusion of order where disorder still remains. May it be possible for instance that the mental state called schizophrenia is a symptom and not a primary disease with no more right to call itself a diagnosis than amnesia has; and like amnesia may it not turn out to be sometimes due to psychiatric cause and sometimes to organic disease? What proportion of mental illness will ultimately be found to have an organic basis? It may be years before such questions can be answered; all one can say at the moment is what Sherlock Holmes said of a very difficult problem: "It opens a pleasing field for intelligent speculation."

# V

## *Is baldness psychological?*

Published in *Clinical Excerpts* April-June 1951

A psychological explanation for baldness is not a surprising thing because it is now the fashion for psychiatrists to put forward mental causes for those illnesses where physical mechanisms have not yet been found – for instance, peptic ulcer, rheumatism, and others. Szasz and Robertson,[1] a psychoanalyst and psychiatrist, watching their patients' expressions decided that bald men looked more tense than non-bald men; from this observation they worked out "a new integrated theory of baldness."

Briefly, they account for baldness thus: a man has a hidden anxiety and a defensive attitude to life. This gives him "a rigid expression, often noticeable as a fixed smile or a toothy smile." Now, as there is a close association between face and scalp movements (both in nerve supply and development), the chronic tonicity of the facial muscles is reflected in chronic scalp tension, which leads to blood-vessel-pinching effects from shearing stresses on the sub-cutaneous tissues of the scalp and consequently to loss of hair. In other words, the man who persistently "puts a brave face on it" is at the same time starving his hair of its blood supply. Wilhelmina Stitch wrote: "It is easy enough

---

[1] Szasz T S, Robertson A M. *Arch Derm Syph Chicago* 1950; **61**: 34-48.

to be pleasant when life goes by like a song, but the man worth while is the man who will smile when everything goes dead wrong." Perhaps these words, so often hung in poker work upon a living room wall, may have unwittingly caused a good many hairs to be shed, for the "smile when everything goes dead wrong" is just that rigid smile which Szasz and Robertson accuse of causing that scalp distortion which leads to baldness; indeed, a famous marching song of the Great War may have produced many bald soldiers, and if we had our songs first vetted by psychiatrists (as perhaps we should) we might be bidden: "Pack up your troubles in the old kit bag and relax, relax, relax." They quote Wilhelm Reich,[1] who considers such smiles "a somatic character armour." "The psychological defences of a neurotic personality which serve as a protection from feelings of insecurity and anxiety." They also point out that tightening of the scalp may occur with a defensive attitude to life just as animals that fight with their teeth draw back their ears when savage to prevent them from being torn by their antagonists (Darwin)[2] and tighten their scalps to prevent their opponents seizing a loose piece of skin. In other words, the bald individual may be one who has tightened his scalp lest fate should take a nip at it, and ordinary alopecia may represent the result of a chronic and concealed snarl at life.

This is an intriguing idea and ingeniously worked out, but it is wise to remember Clifford Allbutt's words, "the use of hypotheses lies not in the display of ingenuity, but in the labour of verification," and much more convincing evidence would have to be forthcoming for the theory to become widely accepted. At the start the original observation that bald men wore fixed expressions might be tested more

[1] Reich W. *Character analysis.* 2nd ed. New York: Orgone Institute Press, 1945.
[2] Darwin C. *The expressions of the emotions in man and animals.* New York: Appleton and Co, 1898.

scientifically by confronting the psychiatrists with a large number of photographs of faces which had their scalps concealed and seeing if they could pick out the bald heads by studying their expressions. Some explanation would also have to be found for the fact that people with one sided facial tics are not observed to have unilateral baldness, although the shearing stresses on the scalp from repeated grimacing must be much greater than those due to a fixed tense expression. The professional strong man too – for ever rippling his pectoral muscles at the circus – might be expected to epilate his sternal region by a similar mechanism, but the hairy chests of such persons are in fact proverbial.

Only two things about ordinary baldness seem to be agreed upon by all observers. Firstly, that it is almost unknown in women, and secondly, that it is often hereditary. Szasz and Robertson manage to fit these observations neatly into their scheme. They attribute women's immunity to baldness to the thicker fat padding in their scalps, which protects the blood vessels against shearing stress (it has been shown that testosterone accounts for the thinner fatty layer in men, and J B Hamilton[1] claimed to produce baldness in eunuchs by giving testosterone). They account for the genetic factors in baldness by saying they predispose to certain skull shapes which favour the development of greater tension of the scalp, or possibly by "determining affinities for more archaic kinds of muscular expression." The second idea is the more intriguing because it suggests that if our inward tension gets the better of us we might revert to an archaic expression with teeth bared and ears drawn back and so begin to get thin on top. Looking at distinguished doctors at a medical meeting it is hard to take this view when we note those placid professional faces which are so often topped by polished domes, but perhaps they may have borne

[1] Hamilton J B. *Am J Anat* 1942; **71**: 451-80.

more archaic expressions in the past. Certainly the schoolboy who bids his companion to restrain his temper says "keep your hair on," and if we are to believe Szasz and Robertson this boyish phrase is no meaningless expression but a medical warning based on psychiatric theory.

Szasz and Robertson attempted to confirm their theory by electromyographic studies of bald and non-bald men. They measured the electrical activity of the occipitalis, expecting the bald subjects to show a continuous action of this muscle, but the bald men were able to relax their scalps as easily as their better covered colleagues. No significant difference in the electromyograms of the two groups was found, but the record voltage (over 1 volt) was registered by a non-bald man wiggling his ears. Despite the negative results of this experiment the authors feel that further research should be done to verify their theory. They suggest submitting the bald subject to more searching procedures, but one cannot help feeling that if a bald man knew that there was a plan to cut the nerves to his scalp, inject radio-active substances into the blood vessels of his hair, fix electrodes to his head throughout the night, and finally to psychoanalyse him, he might develop such a degree of inward tension and such a distortion of the normal facial expression as to interfere materially with the proper scientific conduct of the experiment. Perhaps the average bald man would prefer to buy himself a hat.

# VI

## *Some books are to be tasted . . .*

. . . others to be swallowed, and some few to be chewed and digested
—Francis Bacon

Most of the ones Asher reviewed seem to have belonged to the first category.

Muddy waters may look deeper than they are, and a muddy style lends a certain profundity to this book.

*

Despite the traditional belief that psychiatrists all write obscure nonsense, the psychiatric contributions here . . . are all particularly clear and concise. Moreover, when there is not much to say about a thing, they do not try to conceal the gap by plugging it with wordy vapourings, but simply write very little about the matter.

*

As the book is for general practitioners, to provide them with so much detail and so many references seems rather like giving the complete 16-volume *Oxford Dictionary* to a foreign tourist.

*

Professor Wintrobe, dealing with haematology, certainly knows what he is talking about; but I am not sure that his readers will.

*

Quite a high proportion of the few facts in the book are correct and the pictures are cleverly drawn.

★

Like many others who feel uncomfortable in the world of sense, he tries to sell us tickets to the land of nonsense. The journey is difficult and the destination obscure.

★

This book says, in effect, that many elderly, fat, hairy ladies have thick fronts to their skulls and nobody really knows why.

★

# VII

## *The use of statistics in medicine*

Published in the *Journal of the Student American Medical Association*
April 1956 and adapted from an address given before a meeting of the
Royal Statistical Society on 23 May 1954 at Westminster Hospital
Medical School. Asher spoke in support of a motion which favoured
the increasing use of statistics in all branches of medicine. The motion
was carried unanimously.

I am not a statistician, nor have I leanings toward statistics. I
am a general physician largely ignorant about them, yet
aware of the need to use statistical thinking in medicine.

I believe many doctors distrust statisticians because they
don't understand them. Others admire them for the same
reason. In this respect statistics could almost be grouped
with psychiatry, T S Eliot, and Christopher Fry. The
difference is that with a little trouble one can find out what
statisticians are trying to do despite the abstruseness of their
symbols and techniques.

First of all, statisticians, as I understand their attitude
toward medicine, try to study medical facts in a numerical
way. Whether they are studying clinical results or vital
statistics, they are seeking to determine whether or not the
figures are likely to have occurred by chance. They always
start their calculations by assuming that a numerical result
did occur by chance and by estimating the likelihood of its

occurring in that way. When they find that it is extra-ordinarily unlikely that some results arose by chance they express this fact by various symbols which accurately represent degrees of likelihood. In other words they answer the question, "Is this a fluke or not?" But they never give us a definite yes or no – they say merely whether it is improbable or likely to be a fluke.

Now, just as a doctor studying obesity weighs his patients rather than subdividing them into fat, stout, partly covered, and well covered, so a statistician instead of using terms like highly improbable or pretty likely gives the odds against a result being a fluke. If they find it 20 to one against a fluke they call this significant. If they used the nomenclature of the race track and shouted out "20 to one against fluke" it might be easier for the layman, but instead of this they say $p > 0.05$ – in other words, five in 100 chances of this happening by chance.

Secondly, statisticians help us to study results influenced by multiple factors and assess the effect of one of them. For instance, if there are two groups of patients, one treated and the other not, it might be that one group contained more old people or more ill people than the other, which, of course, might corrupt the results. The statistician with his mastery of figures can make allowances for these disturbing influences and allow the groups to be fairly compared even though they differ in some particulars.

Thirdly, statisticians can give enormous help in the planning of clinical trials. They have various techniques for arranging groups of treated and untreated patients so that they are easy to compare and likely to give information. It is the statistician who has taught us how properly to avoid the ever present factor of emotional bias by using inert control tablets indistinguishable from their active counterparts and concealing the key to their identity from everyone concerned with the experiment. Even today, clinical trials are often done without this elementary precaution and thus become virtually worthless. The effects of suggestion are much greater than might be imagined. In an experiment I once conducted, more than 90% of the group got some relief of pain from a dummy pill and more than 50% obtained complete relief.

Here's another vivid example of the effect of suggestion. When an American town announced it would introduce fluoride into its water supply on a particular date, hundreds of angry housewives called the authorities on the appointed day to complain that their tea was undrinkable, their baths discoloured, and their goldfish dying. It was only then the authorities disclosed that no fluoride had yet been introduced. In eliminating emotional bias in experiments, statisticians have perhaps made their greatest contribution to clinical medicine.

The increased use of statistics in all branches of medicine can be extremely beneficial. Here are some of the many ways the profession can benefit from their use.

By evolving the technique of controlled clinical trials the statisticians help the effective drugs to be recognised early.

Statisticians can save the country endless sums of money by their critical assessments of new and fashionable remedies. For instance, when a wave of enthusiasm for antihistamine drugs was starting to sweep the country the Medical Research Council, aided by statisticians, were soon able to demonstrate their uselessness and stem the rising tide of prescriptions. If statistically controlled trials had been undertaken when vitamins were first discovered, England might have saved a large proportion of the two million pounds annually spent on them.

By studies of the relation of one set of figures to another, statisticians can establish hitherto unrecognised causes for disease. For instance, the importance of German measles in pregnant mothers as a cause of congenital deafness and other afflictions in their offspring – a discovery which may materially reduce these tragedies.

By their studies of the laws of chance statisticians can give the clinician an insight into the inaccuracy of blood counts. The doctor is inclined to think the laboratory worker counts the number of red cells in a cubic millimetre of blood. The statistician, however, points out how much depends on chance – the chance of how many cells happen to land on particular squares in a counting chamber. For instance, if there are four million red cells in a cubic millimetre of blood there is a chance, though a rare one, that an accurately performed count would give the figure as three million. Realisation of this makes the clinician more forgiving of the apparent vagaries of the haematologist.

Statistics allow the accurate study of things which have multiple causes and whose causes are subject to strong emotional bias. Take the relation between smoking and cancer of the lung: the accurate assessment of this is possible only with the aid of statistical technique. Smoking is so common that there would be more smokers than non-smokers in any disease group. Emotional bias is so strong that a prejudiced investigator might easily obtain a heavier smoking history from people he knew had cancer of the lung. Lung cancer can certainly occur in non-smokers. Certain kinds of cancer favour one sex, and smoking is commoner among men than women. All these and other facts have to be taken into account, and their influence either allowed for or eliminated when the problem is studied. The work of Richard Doll and Bradford Hill[1] was a model of the dispassionate controlled statistical investigation of a complex relationship.

Statisticians many times will open the eyes of doctors to the power of nature in effecting a cure. In diseases such as

[1] Doll R, Hill A B. *Br Med J* 1950; iii: 739-46.

peptic ulcer or rheumatoid arthritis the brilliant results obtained by treatment are so often obtainable with comparable frequency by the careful administration of nothing at all three times daily after meals. By their insistence on proper control of clinical trials, the statistician has drawn attention to the high incidence of spontaneous recovery in certain illnesses, recoveries so often claimed by the doctor as being due to his treatment. The effect of statisticians on doctors, therefore, can be to disturb their complacency, to increase their modesty, and to add to their admiration of nature. All these should be welcome influences to the physician.

Having presented some cogent arguments in favour of the use of statistics in medicine I shall now try to demolish some of the common arguments used by those who attack statisticians. Bernard Shaw once said that it was easy to show by statistics that the wearing of a top hat increases the size of the waistband. That type of argument is commonplace, but it is exactly what a statistician would not be able to show. If a statistician studied the waistbands of two groups of persons, one top hatted, the other cloth capped, the first thing he would study would be whether the groups were comparable in other relevant respects such as income, dietary habits, and so on.

Statisticians are many times referred to as men of science without any heart. They are typed as cold, hard, humourless men who deal only with figures, who regard patients not as individuals but as numbers, and who never display emotion or arouse laughter. It has been said that if a statistician was told of the vision of Jacob's ladder he would display no interest until he knew the number of rungs.

My experience of statisticians is that they have as much charm and display, as much sympathy and humour, as anyone else. Indeed, one of the funniest articles I ever read was called "First Steps in Statistics" and was written by C L

Oakley,[1] a statistician. At the time this story was written workers from the Institute of Psychical Research were investigating a legend of the Brocken mountain. The legend was that by use of suitable spells and the use of bats' blood, soot, and honey, a virgin he goat could be converted into a young man by a maiden pure in heart. In this article, Oakley's brilliant analysis of the possibilities of measuring purity in heart and the design of experiments to estimate the mean he goat conversion rate and other matters was one of the wittiest bits of nonsense I have ever read.

Another point that is sometimes made against statisticians is to assume that they are trying to infiltrate medical provinces where they are unwanted. Some doctors regard them as foreigners trying to invade the sacred ground of medicine and contaminating the pure realms of clinical observation with outlandish symbols. That is not my experience. Most statisticians are against an excessive use of statistics in medicine and complain that people sometimes want to use them when there is no need for it.

Those who argue against the use of statistics often say that the statistician is expressing only common sense in an obscure mathematical form. Statisticians admit that this is sometimes true. Usually when something can be expressed in a numerical way it is an aid to more precise and accurate thinking and comparisons can more easily be made. Clinicians, if there are no statisticians to harry them into the use of figures, develop a terminology which can be just as obscure and far less informative than mathematical language. If there is no evidence that a treatment does any good but it does not seem to be harmful, the clinicians report, "Results have so far proved encouraging." If the treatment appears to do slight harm the report is, "Further work on this treatment is required before its efficacy can be assessed." If

[1] Oakley C L. *University College Hospital Magazine* 1943: **28**: 16.

the treatment is frankly harmful they say, "Results have not hitherto proved encouraging."

Common sense is not an adequate substitute for a knowledge of statistics because the interpretation of numerical results is not always obvious or easy. For example, if it were found that 1% of hospital patients in England had pernicious anaemia and only 0·3% in India, it might seem obvious that pernicious anaemia was three times commoner in England when compared with India. However, pernicious anaemia is a disease of elderly people, and because there is a smaller chance of becoming elderly in India, due to the higher mortality rate there, the chances of developing pernicious anaemia may be correspondingly diminished even though the natural incidence is the same. Take an example from a recently published paper. An investigator showed that of 200 epileptic subjects 24% had had infantile convulsions in childhood, whereas of 200 normal controls only 2% had been so afflicted. From this the investigator argued that convulsions in childhood presaged epilepsy in adult life and that any child with infantile convulsions should be given anticonvulsant drugs. The fallacy in this example is certainly not obvious to one untrained in statistical thinking. Actually, the incidence of epilepsy in the population (which is one in 400) has to be considered. Among 40 000 people, therefore, there would be 100 epileptics, 24 of whom had convulsions. But also among those 40 000 people there would be 800 people (2% of 40 000) who had had infantile convulsions but were not epileptics. If this argument were accepted it would mean treating 800 normal people, all but 24 of whom were innocent of epilepsy – in other words, submitting 32 normal children to prolonged anticonvulsant therapy in order to be sure of treating one epileptic early in life.

No, common sense is not enough. Obvious conclusions can be fallacious. A certain amount of statistical knowledge helps prevent doctors from indulging in faulty numerical reasoning and, more important, helps to stop them from leaping into print armed with a sword which is numerically glistening, but statistically blunt. If a doctor thinks he has discovered something important he must ask himself before he publishes, "How likely is this a fluke?" It is here that statisticians can give him an answer and so save him the indignity of seeing his ideas refuted, as well as save patients from useless treatment.

We must, however, realise the limitations of statistics. They can never answer the question, "Does this do that?" All they tell us is, "If this doesn't do that then there is only a one in a hundred chance of getting these results." Rare chances do occur, and statisticians would be the first to admit that undue reverence must not be attributed to statistically significant results. Statistics answer questions about probability, not about certainty.

*Summary*

I have tried to show what statisticians do and what they cannot do. I have pointed out how they can be useful to doctors, how they can help them interpret results where there are multiple factors at work, and how statisticians can tell how likely it is that a scientist's results are due to chance, thus stopping them from publishing nonsense.

# VIII

## Stepping on the gas

Extract from "Picador's Column" published anonymously in *Medical World* 1963

As a student I rather fancied myself as an anaesthetist, and when the instructor left me in charge for a while I enjoyed the feeling of power as I surveyed the row of bubbling bottles and moved the chromium plated levers of the Boyle's machine. The patient was utterly at my mercy: I could make him breathe fast or slow, or turn him pink or blue at will. If I wanted to, I could kill him. Even the surgeon had to wait till I said he could start. If the first anaesthetic I gave after I qualified had gone differently I might be a consultant anaesthetist today, instead of a consultant physician.

Soon after passing my finals I got on the house as emergency officer, which meant deputising for anyone who was away. My first job was to deputise for the senior resident anaesthetist and give an anaesthetic for Mr Gladwyn Gullet, the senior ENT surgeon. He was a vast man with hairy hands, who addressed everybody as "Laddie." He could take out more than 30 pairs of tonsils in a morning with the guillotine, and opened retropharyngeal abscesses holding a child upside down in one hand and opening the abscess with the talon like index fingernail of the other. He kept it sharp for this purpose.

When I arrived he was waiting for me. He wanted to

49

remove some aural polypi on an outpatient. The conditions were not the same as those where I gave my student anaesthetics. There was no quiet anaesthetic room for the induction, but a large room full of bustling nurses and sisters, with Mr Gullet watching over me. He had already had the room darkened so he could see better into the ear, and I could just see my patient was a middle aged woman.

The anaesthetic apparatus was quite different from the Boyle's machine I was used to – no chromium plated levers and bubbling bottles, simply a cylinder of nitrous oxide on the floor, controlled by a foot valve and supplying a rubber bag and mask. "Controlled" isn't quite the right word – "influenced by" would be more accurate. You had to stick your foot in a kind of cage and twist your ankle round when you wanted to open the valve. In practice the cylinder skidded on the stone floor, and the whole thing turned round. So the trick was to twist clockwise till the apparatus got a certain momentum, and then suddenly twist in the other direction and hope your ankle ligaments were strong enough. If they were there was a sudden roar as the valve opened suddenly and the bag swelled with alarming speed.

I investigated these hazards before starting on the patient, while Mr Gullet stood and watched. When I produced a particularly powerful snort of gas and the bag distended almost to bursting, he facetiously put his fingers in his ears and hid under the operating table. Mercifully the patient had her eyes bandaged and her polyps made her fairly deaf, so she was quite calm and willing when I finally subdued the machine and put the mask over her face. Mr Gullet picked up a steel snare and stood waiting by the ear hole rather as if he was a terrier waiting for a rat to pop out. The patient took it like a lamb, without any trace of struggling or noise, and soon, from her steady regular breathing, I knew she was well under; I gave her another half minute for luck – I didn't want Mr Gullet to make any more jokes about my anaesthetics.

At last, when I felt quite sure of her I very cautiously lifted one eyelid to test her corneal reflex. As my finger moved gently towards her eyeball a loud triumphant cry rang through the room: "Peep-boh! I can see you, doctor!" It came from the patient. Never since then have I felt really attracted to anaesthesia as a profession.

# IX

## *Noise*

Published in the *Central Middlesex Hospital Magazine*

The question of the noisiness of this hospital was brought up for discussion at a recent staff meeting. The discussion was surprisingly enthusiastic. Almost every member had a pet noise which caused him especial irritation, and everyone agreed that there ought to be more consideration given to achieving quietness in hospitals. There is no doubt that people work less efficiently when there is a noise going on and also become more irritable. Also it is certain that ill people are more sensitive to noise, and so are patients who are going under an anaesthetic. For these and many other reasons it is worth considering some of the causes of hospital noise and thinking about methods of dealing with them.

The nature of hospital life requires that part of the community sleep while others are awake. All night workers ought to be more aware of their comrades who are sleeping (or trying to sleep) within earshot and adjust their behaviour accordingly. This applies not only to doctors and night nurses but to porters and kitchen workers. Those working by day should pity the poor night worker who, after spending the night shouting, laughing, slamming doors, and banging trays is, when daybreak comes, quite exhausted by his efforts and needs a good sleep. Seriously though, both day and night workers make much more noise than they need to and could do each other good service by conscious quietness. It is in the manipulation of crockery, feet, vocal cords, and bedpans that adjustments could most reasonably be made. Crockery is difficult to manage, and though the plastic industry may later oblige with clatter free crockery, at present gentle handling is the only way to reduce noise and breakages. Feet are very important, and all hospital workers should, like Agag, walk delicately. It is interesting that doctors in charge of guardsmen, who have to stamp on parade to make an impressive noise, have shown that quite a number of fractured metatarsals follow this custom. So "come and trip it as you go on the light fantastic toe," and you may save yourself a fractured foot as well as saving others a disturbed sleep. Squeaking shoes are almost incurable despite many traditional remedies, and if you are unfortunate enough to have some it is best to use them only out of doors. As regards vocal cords the problem is almost insoluble, for nearly everyone seems to feel at their chattiest when walking along corridors or going upstairs, and it is in similar situations that everyone wishes to laugh heartily. If only we could imbue the passages and stairs with the same hushed atmosphere that pervades an operating theatre it would be splendid. Bedpans are a source of much clanging and rattling. The metallic brand used here consist of a hollow handle attached to a gong, and when several are wheeled upon a trolley the clangour is like a smithy. More gentle handling of these articles is the only solution unless we take a tip from the catalogue for the Naval Stores, where under the heading "pots" we find: "Pots – round, red, rubber, lunatic." The trolleys often make a squeaking noise which drowns the rattle of their burden, and here a little oil makes a dramatic difference. A squeaking trolley should be considered a slur on a ward.

The structure of hospital buildings is closely related to the noise that goes on in them. Firstly, the battering from nearby bombs and rockets have left many minor deformities of doors and cupboards, which are hard to shut or else swing open spontaneously. Shortage of supplies and repair staff have increased this difficulty. Secondly, in the design of the buildings attention is not always paid to their noise producing qualities. The John Tate maternity block is famed for its hyper-resonance; and in its capacious and hygienic spaces each sound echoes and re-echoes so that the cacophony of crockery blends with the banging of doors, and the mewling and puking of the babies is drowned by the jangle of wrangling bedpans. The kitchen should not be open to the main corridor as at present, and the floor could have a quieter covering such as the excellent rubbery matting along the main hospital corridor.

Much more could be written on the various noises, but it is hoped that this brief outline may help to make people a little more noise conscious. We should strive to eliminate noise as successfully as we have recently eliminated ants.

# X

## *Intracranial and extracranial computers*

Published in the *Middlesex Hospital Journal* December 1966

It sounds unreasonable to ask a child of six to count more than 200 changes of pressure within half a second by transmitting them through a system of levers to a vibrating spiral of fluid and observing the electrical impulses these vibrations excite in a given conductor.

It sounds even more unreasonable to ask that child, without using pencil and paper, to calculate the number of pressure changes per unit time, then to multiply that figure by two, and express its answer by adjusting two vibrating strands at the end of a wind tunnel so that the frequency of their oscillations is equal to the product of their calculations.

But human intracranial computers are so efficient that children can manage such feats long before they are six: they pick up tunes, and having high voices usually sing them an octave above the original pitch – that is, doubling the frequency. It is all done without instructions by the use of the built in cerebral computer provided; this contains the cumulative data of the innumerable, and sometimes rather trying experiments carried out with the vocal apparatus during most of the waking hours since birth.

It is hard to appreciate the performance of the human intracranial computer because most of its functionings never reach the consciousness of its owner, and it stores data in a very different code from that used in conscious thinking, where synthetic symbols such as words and numbers play a large part. Moreover, it provides answers without giving any hint of the calculations behind them.

A child can sing an octave above a note it hears long before it understands numbers or the frequency relation of octaves; yet the sound waves must have been "counted" in the sense of "registered accurately" if the vocal cords are correctly adjusted to move at exactly twice the frequency. The intracranial computer is "acting on information received" as policemen say, but unlike the policeman's notebook the record cannot be inspected. It is clear the notation is not concerned with numerals, and the information is filed under "how high?" rather than "how often?" or "how many?" Yet the record is really a coded form of numbering, as a note of given pitch can be expressed as a number by consulting a table of frequencies. A child that deviates no more than a third of the interval between the correct note and those on either side of it is numerically accurate within 2%.

Since frequencies cannot be counted without smoked drums and time markers, one would not expect to find any numeral basis underlying their registration. Yet even those things which *are* amenable to counting seem to be mentally recorded without any numeral basis. If I carry a tray downstairs I know when I have reached the landing, although I don't count the steps and I could not tell you how many there are.

*Mental geiger counters*

Here is quite a good example: when I tell you, you will notice in this paragraph I started writing à la *Hiawatha*, and although these words are printed as in prose with no division marking one line from another, I am confident in saying syllables are being numbered by your mental Geiger counters, checking that the stronger accents come whenever eight are counted; and it must be eight exactly, or they will detect the error, for instance this one which makes you feel most uncomfortable.

Back to normal rhythm now, to point out that throughout that paragraph you rapidly and accurately totted up groups of eight syllables. You were not consciously counting, you only were conscious of rhythm. You may not have known the number of syllables per line in *Hiawatha*, but you knew if it was right or not. If you locate the end of each poetic line in that paragraph using only the sense of rhythm you will probably find you are quicker than if you use numbering.

The computering activities of the brain extend far beyond unconscious counting and provide the owner with the fruit of every kind of stored information. Unfortunately, they issue fruit only – not the information. They have extracted the fruit (that is, worked out a conclusion from the facts) before passing the result to you. They tell you *what* the answer is, rather than *why* it is. If you try to write down how you tell a dog from a cat you may agree. A motorist meeting traffic lights which show only the amber light may apply the brake and put the gear in neutral without consciously *knowing* the red light will follow; he does it automatically. If he is asked when he takes his driving test what the sequence of lights is, he may be stumped, even though in practice he would be likely to drive quite well. It is a mark of experience to do things automatically and unconsciously.

The worst of examinations is that they test for conscious knowledge, though experienced people performing activities such as driving cars or diagnosing diseases may perform very well (and possibly better) without it. The experienced clinician is expected to pass on to medical students the observations he uses to make a diagnosis. In fact he can rarely manage to do this.

If illnesses were as common as cats and dogs we might distinguish between them with equal ease, relying on our computered unconscious faculties to provide the answer and without knowing how they obtained it. In fact we probably use such methods with very common conditions: for example, have you ever been *taught* to recognise dropsy by the "shine" of the skin? I don't think I was; and I don't believe many textbooks mention it. Now you come to think of it, will you agree that at the bedside "shine" is one of the first things to suggest there is oedema? Do you admit that as soon as you lift the bed clothes and see that pale shiny tissue, you press a confirmatory thumb into it to make a pit? Of course you do. It does not matter a halfpenny whether you have been taught about "shine" or whether you are conscious of observing it, because as soon as you have been in the wards for a week or so this fact will have been incorporated in the data processing of your intracranial computer.

There must be many other things, seen rather than noticed, known rather than realised, which help in bedside diagnosis. Many of them would be hard to put into words even if we were aware of them: the diminished space between the chin and the sternum in those with emphysema; the increased glitter in the eyes of a thyrotoxic patient (a factor independent of the lid retraction or exophthalmos, or both); the opening and shutting hand of the man describing his anginal pain, and so on.

The alternative method of feeding clinical data into the intracranial machinery is to code them into words which can be fed into the apparatus in the form of lectures or text-books. ("Coding" is a sadly apt term usually.) This method is far less satisfactory than the other, but words are easier to come by than clinical material, and knowledge absorbed in verbal form is already processed for examination use and therefore the more valuable to students, though far less useful for doctors. For instance, students are not only told that oedema pits but also taught that myxoedema does not pit. They might thus hope to discover hypothyroidism by finding a patient who was apparently swollen with dropsy and then noticing it would not pit. I doubt if any clinician has ever diagnosed myxoedema in this way; the two kinds of swelling are so unlike each other; moreover myxoedematous patients often have a little dropsy, enough to make the swollen tissues pit in dependent parts, so the test would be of little use.

### Confirming the severe case

On the same subject, it is traditionally taught that the slow pulse of myxoedema would help to distinguish it from other conditions, whereas in fact bradycardia is rare in hypothyroidism except in the very advanced cases. Even in these it does not contribute much to the *making* of the diagnosis; it joins a diagnosis already made in confirming the severity of the condition, in this sort of way: "Good heavens! What a very severe case of myxoedema I see here. Yes undoubtedly," – taking up the patient's hand – "she has the dry scaly skin and the corpse like coldness. I should think we might even get bradycardia here."

The value of bradycardia in diagnosing myxoedema is similar to that of the classic "soft putty like eyeball" of diabetic coma. It occurs all right, but you get it only when the condition is so advanced that you have already made the diagnosis before you elicit the sign, and you elicit it only if there is a student to display it to. A man has to be pretty severely dehydrated before his eyeballs start drying up, and it means the patient is pretty far gone if they are noticeably softened and that the diagnosis ought to have been made long ago before he got so bad.

You, as a student (I find it easier to write this article assuming that you are one) may feel that consultants and registrars ought to tell you how they *really* make their diagnoses, but that would be almost impossible. The more experienced you are, the better you do things and the less you know how you do them. You just explain to me how you can distinguish between a youth of 15 and a young man of 25; then you may understand. It is quite possible you would mention things such as the fact that the epiphyses of the shoulder and wrist fuse at the age of 18 and those of the elbow at 20, or perhaps go on to refer to the development of the pubic hair and genitals, even though any commissionaire at the doorway of a cinema where an X film is being shown is expected to make a pretty reliable decision without the use of radiology or exposure of the pudenda.

The reason why things such as pitting, slowness of the pulse, soft eyeballs, and fused epiphyses appeal so strongly to both the teacher and the exam answerer is that they are cut and dried, whereas (as I often used to remark to students in my teaching days) human beings and the illnesses that afflict them are joined and damp.


*Machines versus brains*

So much for intracranial computers. Efficient but enigmatic in action, how do they compare with their mechanical extracranial counterparts? Are transistors superior to synapses? There is no doubt that electric computers will be increasingly used in most branches of medicine: they can store a greater number of data and with greater accuracy than the human brain. To what extent will machines supersede brains? This is a matter about which people feel strong emotions. The allure of the technical and transistorised and the appeal of the elaborate and the esoteric, combined with the prestige value of computers, assures their popularity with one kind of person. The fact that computers are not equipped with souls damns them in the eyes of another.

I have never regarded the possession of a soul as being of equal importance to that of a stethoscope and ophthalmoscope in medical work, but despite that I regard the present vogue for computers with cautious scepticism. I imagine that computers will be used largely to store information derived from countless clinical records and to detect significant associations between the various items. Highly important associations may exist for many years before they are noticed.

Three examples from the last one or two decades are the relation of deafness to maternal rubella, that between neonatal oxygen administration and infantile blindness, and the association between pink disease and the ingestion of mercurial teething powders. Computers with faultless memories and flawless powers of correlation could be expected to pick out such things immediately, whereas doctors, using only their intracranial computers, failed to notice them for many years. Ah yes; but did the doctors fail because of their intracranial apparatuses or was their failure due to lack of data? Had they known which children were being given teething powders it seems likely they would quite soon have noticed the association with pink disease. The material you collect to think over is just as important as the way you think over it. Both human brains and mechanical brains are dependent on the data fed into them.

It seems unlikely in their present form that much information of value could be distilled from the enormous quantity of data already contained in hospital clinical notes, if it could be analysed by computers. The problem of deciphering and extracting the data and processing it into computer fodder would be formidable. If you have ever searched a lot of hospital records to find out if measles prevents migraine or to decide whether twins are predisposed to torticollis, you will know that only in exceptional cases can you establish from the notes whether a patient definitely suffered from migraine or torticollis, and in those rare instances you hardly ever find it recorded whether the patient had measles or if he was a twin.

To gather suitable massed clinical data for a computer it would be necessary for every patient to answer an elaborate standardised questionnaire. The problems involved in designing this, in ensuring its accurate completion, and in dealing with the effects of its interference with established routines might be almost insuperable.

Even after completing such a project the results might turn out to be disappointing at first because human brains have the advantage over mechanical ones that the conclusions derived from the data provided are selected and scrutinised below the level of consciousness and those that are obviously valueless are screened off before reaching serious consideration. For example, you as a student have never pondered deeply on the fact that men never appear to suffer from postpartum haemorrhage and that under the age of 2 alcoholic cirrhosis of the liver is almost unknown. A mechanical brain would announce such conclusions as portentously as those of graver significance. Even if the obvious and useless conclusions could be screened off in some way, the remaining results would be of very uncertain value. An astute mechanical brain would not take long to observe that the children of habitual opium smokers practically never develop erythroblastosis fetalis, and also that children who habitually sucked dummy teats in their infancy were more than averagely prone to rickets. A human brain would observe in addition that as opium smoking as a habit is largely confined to the Chinese (who are 99% rhesus positive) the first conclusion was not very surprising, and comment on the second by suggesting that the sucking of dummies being found largely among the poor, the fact that poor people have less easy access to food and light might account for it. A computer would not make such disparaging criticisms unless it had been fed with information about the commoner customs of the Chinese and the poor.

*Unappreciated knowledge*

Thinking about that kind of thing makes you more aware of the surprising number of data accommodated in your own brain. Trivial everyday fragments of knowledge lie unappreciated in some remote corner of the cortex or hiding behind some basal ganglion or other, ready to rush into consciousness when they are wanted. You don't even have to call for them. There is really a lot to be said for continuing the use of the intracranial apparatus. Even if you own a computer it is advisable to spend a certain amount of time in thought. I am not disputing that computers have enormous potential value, but it will be many years before they outstrip the performance of the human brain; it is doubtful if they will ever compete with it as regards adaptability, portability, and ease of maintenance. Moreover, intracranial computers are gathering their own data continuously whereas the extracranial variety are dependent on their masters for their data.

As regards their use in diagnosis, I doubt whether they will be of great value. It is perfectly possible to provide by mechanical means a list of the diagnoses which would account for a given collection of symptoms or signs. A simple non-electronic version of such an instrument (called the logoscope) has already been produced by Dr F A Nash. It is something like a slide rule in design. Supposing a diagnostic computer was provided with the four items of data: (*a*) high blood urea, (*b*) red conjunctivae, (*c*) jaundice, and (*d*) muscular pains. It would register Weil's disease (leptospirosis icterohaemorrhagica), which is as far as I know the only diagnosis which would account for them all. Or, to take a surgical example: given (*a*) high intestinal obstruction, (*b*) haematemesis, (*c*) upper abdominal tumour, and (*d*) past gastroenterostomy it would indicate retrograde intussusception through stoma. When there were rather outlandish collections of clear cut symptoms, such as in the two examples, an instrument of this kind could occasionally help an inexperienced man (if he chose the right symptoms to put into it and had elicited them correctly), but few patients oblige with the symptoms it is their duty to have and not many refrain from complaining of those they ought not to have. When I tried to teach the art of medical diagnosis to students, I often used to ask them this riddle from my prep school days: "What runs about farm yards, flaps its wings, lays eggs and barks like a dog? It is difficult isn't it? Have you guessed it? The answer is 'a hen!'" Usually one of the more earnest and innocent of the students would say: "But sir! I don't understand the bit about barking like a dog." "Ah yes. I must explain. That was just put in to make it difficult."

What a silly riddle it is; but if you have had much medical experience you will understand the point of telling it. Patients so often produce an egregious and distracting symptom in addition to the symptoms they ought to have. In fact, because patients as well as hens have a tendency to bark like a dog, I doubt whether any diagnostic machine will be more successful than a sound medical opinion.

I conclude with an experience of mine which seems relevant to the subject of this paper. I wanted to use in a lecture a cartoon I recollected seeing in *Punch* some 30 or 40 years previously. I sent a brief description to the *Punch* editorial office and asked if there was any chance of their finding it. They sent it back to me by return. As they must have published well over 50 000 cartoons during my life-time I was much impressed, and I wrote to thank them, saying what an elaborate system of classifications and indexes and cross references they must have to achieve such a feat. They wrote back to say that all they had was one elderly lady with rather a good memory.

# XI

## *Sir,*

"For letting off steam and entertaining others – write fiery letters in the correspondence columns of the medical journals."—Richard Asher

All these letters, with the exception of the two on attempted suicide, which appeared in the *Lancet* 16 February and 16 March 1963, were addressed to the Editor, *British Medical Journal*.

## *History? or natural history?*

SIR, – Will someone explain what "the natural history" of an illness is? Mr J I Burn and Mr Selwyn F Taylor call their excellent article on thyroid carcinoma (10 November 1962, p 1218) "Natural History of Thyroid Carcinoma," and perhaps they can explain what this means.

"Natural history" in the ordinary way suggests birds, bees, flowers, and animals in the wild, and Gilbert White used the words thus in his famous work *The Natural History of Selborne*. Then the late Professor Ryle produced a stimulating book, *The Natural History of Disease*. The title hinted at years of painstaking study, like that of a naturalist, and suggested a grandeur similar to White's *Selborne* which, with the novelty of the title, may have contributed to the great popularity of the work. But did the words mean anything more than "the course of disease"? Do Mr Burn and

Mr Taylor write on anything other than the "course of thyroid carcinoma"? If the word "natural" has any meaning when applied thus, surely it would imply that *untreated* patients were studied. To know what happens to diseases when doctors do not interfere with them is of vast importance, for the effects of treatment can rarely be judged except by comparing treated and untreated patients. But neither Ryle nor Mr Burn and Mr Taylor confined themselves to untreated patients, and the expression "natural history" is becoming a popular and grandiose synonym for "history." It is no help to the march of science when authors use expressions which sound profounder than their simpler equivalent. Pathologists who feel it sounds too naive to write "this looks like a lymphocyte" will produce: "The appearance is morphologically indistinguishable from a lymphocyte," but they do not gain in dignity thereby. Similarly, if people are going to write about the course of various illnesses would it not be better to avoid this rather pretentious expression "natural history"? – I am, etc,

London w1                                   RICHARD ASHER

## "Anovlar"

SIR, – In their summary on page 78 (14 July 1962), Drs Eleanor Mears and Ellen C G Grant give an admirable digest of their results in an extensive trial on more than 500 women, involving over 2000 cycles, of an oral preparation intended to prevent pregnancy.

Yet there is one omission. They do not say if it prevented pregnancy. I think they should have done, so I write to point out that it did (see main article, foot of p 76). – I am, etc,

London w1                                   RICHARD ASHER

# Attempted suicide

The pair of letters under this title show Asher at his most formidable – expressing something he feels strongly, but doing it with precision and subtle humour. The first one is so lucid that his careful explanation of its meaning in his answer to the psychiatrists who had commented on it is really a laugh at their expense – I wonder if they realised they were being offered the epistolatory equivalent of one of those joke bunches of flowers that squirt water in your face.

SIR, – I share Professor Stengel's doubt (2 February 1963) whether it is practicable for psychiatrists to see all cases of attempted suicide, but I do not share his view that it is necessary or desirable. I have seen nearly all the attempted suicide cases at the Central Middlesex Hospital for 20 years, so my opinions are based on much experience, though they may be wrong.

Some of these cases do need to be seen in hospital by psychiatrists or referred later to their outpatient clinics, but is it right to suggest that every single one *must* see a psychiatrist? Is it right to assume they have not been properly looked after if they do not?

Only a few of these patients really mean to commit suicide, but whatever their intention, they receive the serious label – "attempted suicide." Some of them are just "fed up" and seek a holiday from the tedium of existence by taking a big sleep, and not caring about the risk. Others get in a fix and know that "attempting suicide" brings them help, plus the status of "psychiatric case," whereas other efforts still leave them as "a chap who's got in a jam."

I believe most of these people can be managed safely and

well by a general physician or his registrar, and this has three advantages. Firstly, physicians are more at home with the physical problems of resuscitation. Secondly, some patients prefer to talk with "an ordinary doctor" and feel branded as "a mental case" when under a psychiatrist. When I visit an "attempted suicide" case in someone else's wards (my own wards have realised by now I am not a psychiatrist), I am often asked, suspiciously, if I am a psychiatrist and have heard a sigh of relief when a patient has found I was not; some patients hold a similar attitude to members of the Church. We must not condone the baseless prejudices of the ignorant, yet it is right to take notice of them. Thirdly, in my own hospital, and probably in many others, there are only two or three sessions of a few hours when psychiatrists are on the spot; they are less readily available for these patients than physicians. Moreover they do not lunch with us, so we lose the most valuable means of hearing from our colleagues their opinion on the patients we have asked them to see.

It is a mistake for the Ministry to suggest that a standard practice should be used for a wide variety of cases merely because they can be grouped under the single heading "attempted suicide." It is a tedious platitude to remark that every patient is an individual human being, rather than case no 123, and that he has personal problems each requiring particular management according to the judgment of the doctor in charge. But this platitude needs restating when a directive issued by one regional board asks: "All Hospital Management Committees shall ensure that all cases of attempted suicide brought to their notice are referred for psychiatric advice as early as practicable" or "arrangements should be made for a psychiatric Out Patient appointment."

I refer some of my "attempted suicide" patients to psychiatrists when I think psychiatry may help them, just as

I refer some of my patients with duodenal ulcer to surgeons when I think that surgery will help them. I use my judgment. If I was not allowed to use judgment, but was told by the board, "All cases of duodenal ulcers are to be referred to surgeons as soon as possible," and if I toed the regional line dutifully I might find the life of a physician dull, for some of my other interests might be redirected to other specialists – myxoedema and Marfan's syndrome to mycologists and narcolepsy and neuropathies to neurosurgeons. I prefer to be left alone to decide what to do with my patients, and so I hope do many others.

London W1                          RICHARD ASHER


SIR, – May I thank the various psychiatrists who have commented on the subject of my letter. I do not think we disagree much about facts, but I will clarify a few points where there seems to have been misunderstanding.

Although gain in status ("this man's troubles are important") arises from the seriousness of the patient's act, loss of status ("this man is 'mental'") may occur from his being under a psychiatrist. The first arises from the nature of his act and the second from the nature of his prejudices. I did not think that mentioning the existence of these prejudices would make anyone think I believed them. I do not.

I know some psychiatrists are expert at resuscitation, but I still believe the statement "physicians are more at home with resuscitation" is true; true in the sense that the statement "Men are more at home with machines than women are" would be disputed by few, although there are some exceptions.

I appreciate that if psychiatrists are less readily available than physicians, this does not reflect on the psychiatrists but on those who decide how many of them are needed. Yet, if psychiatrists are available for only, say, eight out of the 168 hours in a week, those patients who are under physicians may get help sooner than those who have to wait for psychiatrists; I thought it fair to list this as a possible advantage.

I agree with Dr Spencer (23 February 1963) that risking life is a serious matter, but I used the words "just fed up" to convey that the reasons for risking it may be trivial (people daily risk their lives by laziness in not bothering to switch off electric current or by impatience at the traffic lights). People who are "just fed up" with trivial annoyances often go and get drunk, but it is doubtful if anyone who gets drunk needs the "assiduous investigation and handling" mentioned by Dr Spencer. Many patients who arrive unconscious from excessive tranquillisers are simply "blind tranquil" as others are "blind drunk." I do not dispute that much care is needed to ensure that no serious purpose lies behind any apparent attempt at suicide; I want only to point out that a surprisingly trivial motive is often found.

I appreciate Dr Pullar-Strecker's support (2 March 1963), but if he is suggesting that physicians endure more misfortunes than psychiatrists do, and are therefore more suited to help fellow sufferers, I do not agree. I believe psychiatrists are more widely exposed to the bitter winds of criticism than physicians are. The ill informed opinions of judges, the misconceptions scattered by the popular press, and the cruelly inappropriate sobriquets which are unkindly applied to them – "trick cyclist," "head shrinker," and so on – such things can hardly fail to make them sensitive and therefore too easily provoked. The tone of their letters suggests that this is so, for I said nothing against psychiatrists in my letter, and yet they all seem to be rather upset.

Dr Stafford-Clark (23 February 1963) asked the purpose of my writing that letter. I gladly explain: it was to suggest that not *all* cases of "attempted suicide" need to be seen by psychiatrists and that physicians could well deal with many of them. Also I wished to expose the foolishness of a regional board trying to impose a particular type of treatment by asking a management committee to enforce it.

I am sorry there seems to be such a wide gulf between psychiatrists and physicians, and that misunderstandings like this arise so easily.

London w1                                                    RICHARD ASHER


## Nocturnal dogs, piscatory cats, Eton College, and alcohol

In April 1960 the *British Medical Journal* published "Clinical Sense," the first of Asher's three Lettsomian lectures delivered at the Medical Society of London in 1959. In it he quoted a passage from a Sherlock Holmes story – or rather, as a correspondent pointed out – misquoted it. There follows an object lesson in getting yourself out of a tight corner and then, with the float-like-a-butterfly-sting-like-a-bee technique, going on to win the round


SIR, – I am guilty of a grave offence. I, for many years a member of the Sherlock Holmes Society of London and recently elected to the council of that distinguished society; I, the author of a short monograph on Sherlock Holmes, not only misquoted from a Sherlock Holmes story but published my vile travesty in print.

Since my friend Dr John Hawksley first pointed out my error to me, I have been waiting for the inevitable public exposure and disgrace. When subsequent issues contained no correction I thought my crime had been undetected and repeated to myself a remark of Holmes's: "Only one important thing has happened in the last three days, and that is that nothing has happened"[1] (another saying which illustrates that negative observations can be important). Now, as I have been exposed in your columns, I had better confess all.

I wrote that passage late at night; the *Memoirs of Sherlock Holmes* was in another room, the *Oxford Dictionary of Quotations* had gone to my wife's bedside with *The Times* crossword, and I wrote on, intending to verify my data next day; but, like the famous dog in the night time, I did nothing. As Dr Box points out, my mistake, vividly though unintentionally, amplifies the point I was making – that it is easy to see what we expect rather than what is there. This makes the offence no more forgivable. "It is a capital mistake," as Holmes remarked, "to theorize before one has data.[2] Insensibly one begins to twist facts to suit theories instead of theories to suit facts."

How can I atone for my carelessness? To accept Holmes's ruling that the offence is "capital" would be incompatible with contemporary restrictions on this form of punishment and the spirit of Sir Ernest Gowers's report. I understand that the BMA library and the editorial offices of the *BMJ* do not possess a copy of the short stories of Sherlock Holmes. This sorry state of affairs clearly needs putting right as soon as possible. Therefore I send with this letter a new copy of *The Complete Short Stories of Sherlock Holmes*: (*a*) to provide a necessary reference work for your editorial offices; (*b*) to provide diversional therapy for your staff at those moments when they may find the burden of medical

[1] Conan Doyle A. *The Sherlock Holmes short stories*. London: John Murray, 1928: 875.
[2] Conan Doyle A. *The Sherlock Holmes short stories*. London: John Murray, 1928: 7.

literature lies specially heavily on them; (c) to atone for the capital mistake of theorising before I had got my data. – I am, etc,

London w1                                      RICHARD ASHER

SIR, – My paper – "Clinical Sense" (2 April 1960, p 985) – referred to human error in observation. Correspondents who have written to you about my paper since then have emphasised this very ably. Dr Valerie Box (7 May, p 1433) got the title of my paper wrong, the title of Conan Doyle's story inaccurate, and the quotation from the story incomplete. Dr R Christopher Howard (21 May, p 1573) referred to the wrong poem (how odd to confuse drowned cats with a distant prospect of Eton College) and even the right poem contains the wrong meaning; my mention of gold glittering among dross was not a quotation of any kind. Dr John Miller (16 April 1960, p 1211) was more accurate, but forgot that alcohol is an anaesthetic; Keats recognised this when he called, "Oh, for a beaker full . . .," explaining that he wished to take enough to "leave the world unseen."

The impervious armour of extensive learning is not possessed by all epistolary gladiators; but at least they can take the trouble to acquire a temporary outfit by visiting the cultural equivalent of Moss Bros – the Public Reference Library. Among quotations they might find there, I commend to them the following: "Read not to contradict and confute, nor to believe and take for granted, nor to find talk and discourse, but to weigh and consider." – I am, etc,

London w1                                      RICHARD ASHER

In his cuttings of this correspondence there is the following note in Asher's handwriting: "Before this was printed I sent (to each of the three people I was replying to) a letter to say I had enjoyed their letters and this haughty tone was purely part of the one-upmanship of correspondence column writing."

## A beginning . . .

Sir, – Dr J S Baker (8 April 1961, p 1038) says it is well
known that anorexia, weight loss, and vomiting are un-
common in pernicious anaemia. He is right. It is well
known. The error in his argument is that he has assumed
that what is well known (that is, generally accepted) is
therefore true. That is not so.

## . . . and an end

I am not criticising the article itself, only your policy in
printing it. If I am wrong in believing that less than 2% of
your readers understand most of the technical terms, I
apologise for unfair criticism, but if I am right I suggest that
you owe it to your subscribers to give them useful, understandable, and practical knowledge instead of allotov-words-
2-obscure-4-any 1 2 succidin-understanding them. – I am,
etc,

London w1                                    RICHARD ASHER

75

# XII

## A case of health

Published in the *British Medical Journal* 15 February 1958

Many cases of unusual illness are described in these columns, so it may make a change if I report a case of unusual health. The lady I describe here is healthy not only in the sense of never being ill but in the more practical fashion of being useful and hard at work for 76 consecutive years with only 10 days' illness. My knowledge of her is purely social. She never consults doctors: "I don't believe in them," she says.

Fanny, as everyone calls her, was aged 90 on 31 January and works as a cook and general servant at a girls' day school in London. She was born on 31 January 1868. She went to school till the age of 13 and then started work in domestic service. Since then she has worked at this profession without any illness or absence from work except for 10 days off in 1932 with bronchitis and severe fatigue after she had been nursing her husband with a fatal illness.

She started her present post 42 years ago; it is both strenuous and responsible. She cooks for 90 people and is also housekeeper to the headmistress. Her average working day is as follows: 6.30 am she gets up and takes her dog for a walk, after which she cooks breakfast for four; 9.30 am goes out shopping for the school; 11 am starts cooking the school lunch ready for 1 o'clock; 1.30 pm receives and sorts the dirty crockery brought down by the children, takes her dog for a walk, and then changes into a black dress and apron for the afternoon. From 2 to 4 pm she is on duty for the front door bell but manages to get a little rest during this time; 4 pm she gets tea ready for the staff of seven teachers; 4.30 pm clears up tea; 7 pm prepares supper for her mistress; 9.30 to 10 pm takes her dog out for an evening walk and then goes to bed.

On Saturdays she does cleaning and polishing. On Sundays she does her washing in the morning and then cooks and serves lunch. She takes the afternoon off and prepares a cold supper for the evening. She stays at the school during the holidays even when her mistress is away, when she is quite alone in the house. She is an alert, spry little woman who moves quickly and vigorously. She enjoys her work, and her mistress, who is devoted to her, regards her as a treasure.

Though many people are very active at 90, it is rather unusual to perform quite so much responsible work at this age and to work at one job so many years without absence through illness. This rare condition of health is probably hereditary – her mother lived to 100, her sisters died at 89 and 86, and her brother is 86.

# XIII

## *Why are medical journals so dull?*

Published in the *British Medical Journal* 23 August 1958

Medical journals are dull; I do not think there is any doubt about that. There are many causes of their dullness; some are curable and some incurable. I do not separate them: this is a short study of the pathology, not a dissertation on the prophylaxis and treatment, of the condition.

### *Wrappers and covers*

Their wrappings are drab and difficult to remove, so the journals accumulate on our desks in inconvenient piles and roll on to the floor. There is little incentive to make the effort of opening them. When opened they have a strong tendency to roll themselves up again.

The covers are as drab as the wrappers. There is nothing on the cover to distinguish one copy from another or to titillate the clinical appetite. There is in some journals a table of contents on the outside page, but the titles are so discouraging that they provide very little incentive for reading the journal, especially to a man already weakened by the effort of unwrapping and correctively rerolling the twisted pages. In other journals the table of contents is hidden among the first few pages of advertisements. Advertisers pay more if their wares are inserted half way through the programme, as in commercial television, and so while hopefully scanning the contents one is interrupted by a vasodilator or a purgative. With the *Proceedings of the Royal Society of Medicine* I have quite often missed something because an advertisement made me think I had finished the list of contents.

## Titles

Many of the titles are unattractive. Without going in for sensationalism an author can try to make his title allure as well as inform. A medical journal is an open market where each salesman must cry his goods if he wishes to get an audience at his stall. A poor title dulls the clinical appetite, whereas a good title whets it. I have called this article "Why are Medical Journals so Dull?" I do not claim this title is specially good, but it is better than "A Study of the Negativistic Psychomotor Reactions induced by Perusal of Verbalized Clinical Material." Titles such as "A Trial of 4.4-Diethyl-hydro-balderdashic Acid in Acute Coryzal Infections" are far better changed to "A New Treatment for Colds."

An important addition to the title should be the author's name, which may attract or repel according to the reputation he enjoys; but medical articles today often appear to be written by committees, and this multiple authorship is highly discouraging to readers. Ten men cannot write an article any more than 10 men can drive a car. The interest evoked by an author's name is diluted by listing all his advisers.

## Wanting in colour

So much for the cover. Now for the inside. The paper is often of poor quality, and coloured pictures are almost unknown. I realise it is economically impossible that this should be otherwise, but medical journals contrast so glumly with the glossy productions of the big drug houses or with women's weeklies.

The advertisements in medical journals are essential to add revenue, but they add little else and seem far less exciting than the advertisements in lay weeklies. Prosperous people in brightly coloured dresses sipping expensive drinks in luxurious liners provide us with happy daydreams of holidays we cannot afford. Advertisements in medical journals are quite the reverse: elderly men in shabby pyjamas hurrying along the passage with urinary frequency. They are not attractive; nor are the other afflicted persons pictured there with tension, hypertension, insomnia, and pain. Humorous advertisements in medical advertising are rare; it might be cheering to see a strip cartoon of the doctor whose practice dwindled because of night starvation but rose with dramatic success after Horlicks; or the physician who found his failure to be elected to fellowship was due to his not using Amplex.

In short, there are many factors which dull the prospect of reading a medical journal even before the letterpress is reached: the wrapping, the unwrapping, the titles, the authors, and the advertisements. There are additional psychological deterrents – the feeling of duty: "I ought to read this for my exams; for my edification; to keep up with my houseman; because my patients will read it in the *Reader's Digest*; or because George will ask me what I think of it. Duty, if one is aware of it, is usually a deterrent, but it is also associated with the idea that a lot of what you don't fancy does you good.

*A tedious duty*

Now for the letterpress itself. It is inevitable that editors have to accept a certain amount of junk both to fill their papers and to avoid giving offence to eminent medical men. For many doctors the achievement of a published article is a tedious duty to be surmounted as a necessary hurdle in a medical career. You have got to get over it, just as you have to dissect a dogfish for the first MB; you don't like it, but it's got to be done. Though the subject of an article is important, it is not much to do with its dullness. I believe that if a man has something to say which interests him, and he knows how to say it, then he need never be dull. Unfortunately, some people have a desire for publication but nothing more. They have nothing to say, and they do not know how to say it. They want to be seen in the *British Medical Journal* or the *Lancet* because it is respectable to be seen there, like being seen in church. They would stand no chance of publication in lay magazines, but the number of medical magazines is so large that every dull dog has his day. Often there seems to be a spate of articles on the same subject: for example, intervertebral discs were all the rage some years ago, whereas hiatus hernia is much in the news today. Other subjects, especially in the correspondence columns, flower, like cacti, every two or three years: for instance, discussions on herpes zoster and chickenpox, or on the correct use of "tropic" and "trophic."

## Good presentation

The dullness of an article depends much on its presentation – that is, the way it is set out, the order in which the facts are put, and the way the diagrams or pictures are arranged. It is astonishing what a difference this makes. For example, here are two ways of setting out one case. A man was crushed by a bombed building, injuring his diaphragm. He consequently developed a right diaphragmatic hernia which resulted in dyspepsia from visceral displacement. Surgical repair of the hernia relieved his symptoms.

That account is factual and accurate, but not especially interesting. Here is the same case as I heard it described by the surgeon at a meeting of a clinical section. He operated on a man who had symptoms of duodenal ulcer, and to his chagrin was unable to deliver the duodenum. At length his exploring hands disappeared into a large hole in the right diaphragm, where he found much intestine. There was no duodenal ulcer. He then reviewed the chest x-ray film and found that the alleged thickened pleura was really hernia and that gas could be (and should have been) recognised in it. As soon as the man came round from the operation a fresh history was taken, and it was found that the pain was nothing like ulcer pain; it had no periodicity (it had been caused by the duodenum being stretched across the lumbar spine). Also, the history of the crush injury was elicited; until then it had not been discovered. The surgeon concluded: "The moral is that one ought to take a history before the operation rather than after it."

You will agree that this second version is live: the first was dead. The first was chronological and factual, yet was tidied up so much that there was no interest left: it had the dullness of a sieved diet.

May I mention a recently published case of my own, "A Woman with the Stiff-man Syndrome"? Here I wrote the account of events not in chronological order but in logical order, starting with my reading an annotation on this syndrome, then my realising I had seen a case of it 10 years previously, then a search for the lady, followed by a review of the notes, and finally a description of her behaviour at a clinical meeting. I thought this would make the article more alive. This device of telling a story by starting in the present and darting to the past and back is far from original, yet to my surprise I received a large number of approving letters and telephone calls praising the way the article was written. I did not know so many people minded about presentation.

The amount of comment produced when trouble was taken to make the presentation as interesting as possible suggests that the average contribution may be rather dull in presentation and that a lively contribution shines like a good deed in a naughty world. I am sure many people writing for medical journals would take more trouble if they knew how much difference it made.

To refer to an article of my own in the above paragraph may suggest I am immodest. That is a risk of using the first person. Yet avoiding "I" by impersonality and circumlocution leads to dullness, and I would rather be thought conceited than dull. Articles are written to interest the reader, not to make him admire the author. Overconscientious anonymity can be overdone, as in the article by two authors which had a footnote: "Since this article was written, unfortunately one of us has died."

An important factor in presentation is the use of diagrams, charts, tables, and so on. I often find that I cannot understand diagrams in medical journals even when I try very hard. I take several minutes identifying the ordinates and sorting out the different types of hatching and shading and their interpretation. Then I usually find I have been looking at fig 1 instead of fig 2. A diagram should be used only if it makes something easier to understand. The purpose of a diagram is not to crowd as many facts as possible into the smallest space.

## Style

Style is what matters most; grammar, syntax, spelling, and punctuation are only useful conventions. They matter very little, nor need we disapprove strongly about improper unions between Greek and Latin or we would have to say dicycle, instead of bicycle. What *does* matter is when doctors write what Ivor Brown calls "pudder" and Sir Ernest Gowers calls "gobbledygook." They clog their meaning with muddy words and pompous prolixity; they spend little time in seeking the shortest, neatest, and plainest way of putting down their meaning. Quiller-Couch, A P Herbert, Ivor Brown, and Sir Ernest Gowers have done a great deal to encourage good writing, but I think Sir Ernest Gowers's *Plain Words* is the best of all. Unfortunately, those who need it most read it least, because anyone taking trouble to buy a book about using English will probably take trouble in writing it: style is largely a matter of taking trouble, though many people wrongly regard it as a gift. The people who write badly do not seem to realise they do, and so do not buy this admirable book.

Here is a sentence from a medical journal: "Experiments are described which demonstrate that in normal individuals the lowest concentration in which sucrose can be detected by means of gustation differs from the lowest concentration in which sucrose (in the amount employed) has to be ingested in order to produce a demonstrable decrease in olfactory acuity and a noteworthy conversion of sensations interpreted as a satiety associated with ingestion of food." All the author meant was: Experiments are described which show that normal people can taste sugar in water in quantities not strong enough to interfere with their sense of smell or take away their appetite.

Lastly, length. Medical articles should, like after dinner speeches, finish before the audience's interest has started to wane. I finish now, pointing out that this paper, like the talk on which it is based, is intended only to provoke discussion. It solves no problems; it only poses them. It is incomplete, inaccurate, and probably irritating; but I hope – and I have spent many hours trying to achieve that end – that it is not dull.

# XIV

## Some Asherisms

"He was perhaps the most memorable epigrammatic arresting medical writer of our time."—FAJ, the *Lancet*

Blind faith in doctors, though convenient, is not always to their benefit.

⋆

A problem is easier to countenance if it has been aired and put into words. I felt rather small recently when a father, thanking me for giving some psychological treatment to his son, said: "I think it's done him a lot of good being able to tell all his troubles to someone. When I was his age I used to tell all my troubles to a large rubber duck, and it seemed a great help. I suppose you're much the same sort of thing." I had not previously considered myself as the therapeutic equivalent of a large rubber duck, and found it both humbling and enlightening.

⋆

Nobody enjoys disease, but there is no doubt that some people enjoy sin. Hence it is easier to treat or prevent disease than to eliminate sin.

⋆

It is not always worth the discomforts of major surgery to get minor recovery.

⋆

People who never wash are less pleasing to examine, but I have never noticed that they seem more prone to disease.

*

Once a man is a doctor he usually does all he can to acquire a dignified uniformity with the remainder of his species.

*

The difference between the maniac and the schizophrenic laugh is – mania and the world laughs with you – schizophrenia and you smile alone.

*

In science and in scientific discussion emotional terms have no place. The poet may say that the fiery blood of Vikings runs in somebody's veins, but the doctor concerns himself with the Wassermann reaction.

*

Nobody can have any kind of relations with a rubber stamp.

*

Gynaecologists are very smooth indeed. Because they have to listen so often to woeful and sordid symptoms they develop an expression of refinement and sympathy.

*

Our function as physicians is to promote the health of those who come to us for help; in our zeal to prolong life let us not, without good cause, lessen their joy in living . . . "a little of what you fancy does you good" . . . a lot of what you do not fancy does you harm.

*

Doctors, like the White Knight, have always felt that once anything is labelled more is known about it; and if a thing is already labelled that does not deter them from applying another label.

*

One knows nothing more about a cat from knowing it is a pussy: an additional name does not mean additional knowledge.

★

You cannot look in the *Medical Directory* and choose a four star or five star doctor, as you might look in the *A A Handbook* and choose a particularly good and well recommended hotel.

★

How well a tranquilliser works
With a believer's ear.
It soothes all sorrows, all that irks
And drives away all fear.

It makes the grip of care unclench
And calms the troubled breast;
'Tis manna to Smith Kline and French
And to the weary rest.

Weak is the effort of my pen
To voice my coldest thought,
But I feel doctors now and then
Prescribe more than they ought.

★

Despair is best treated with hope, not dope.

★

May I wish you happy transfusions which finish with all the blood in the patient and none on the bed, on the floor, or in the doctor's hair.

★

# XV

## Dinner for the Snark

Shortly after the end of the second world war Asher became a member of the Snark club. This had been formed in 1934 by a group of Cambridge medical students, its object being "the glorification of the Snark and its creator." (It is still in existence, its golden jubilee being in May 1984.) The club consists at any one time of 10 members, corresponding to the 10 members of the Snark hunting crew in Lewis Carroll's poem *The Hunting of the Snark* (they are the Bellman, Banker, Baker, maker of Bonnets and Hoods, Boots, Barrister, Broker, Billiard-marker, Butcher, and Beaver). On the departure of the maker of Bonnets and Hoods to New Zealand Asher was elected to replace him "on his own recognisances, as coming from Oxford Circus" (the Middlesex Hospital). When, in April 1966, the *Observer* published a Braintwister puzzle challenging readers to calculate the Snark's dinner time Asher rose to the occasion with his usual panache. Most of what follows is self explanatory. The rest is incomprehensible if, like the Beaver, you have in earlier years taken no pains with your sums.

## The puzzle

### SNARKED

By D St P Barnard

The Baker drew his seventh coat more tightly round his shoulders. It was chilly in that land of shadowy scenes, but

88

his confidence was slowly returning, and he cleared his throat to venture upon a remark as his host munched away at a pawful of greens and soap:

"But your habit of getting up late, you'll agree,
"That you carry too far, for they say
"That you frequently breakfast at five-o'clock tea,
"And dine on the following day."

"There is no reason," remarked the Snark seriously. "I dine only when the three hands of my watch – hour hand, minute hand, and sweep second hand – *exactly* trisect the dial."

"So said our beloved Bellman, but our Butcher declared the thing impossible," replied the Baker.

"Nothing is impossible, returned the Snark sharply. "I have had my watch specially adjusted so that it *is* possible – otherwise how should I know when it is time to dine?" You see, while the hour and minute hands have been left accurately set, the second has been pushed forward just enough, but no more than is absolutely necessary, to enable all three to trisect the dial at some time during the day – and when they do trisect, I dine at *exactly*. . . ."

But at the sight of the railway share which the Baker produced from his pocket in order to note the time down, the Snark, with whiffle of fear, boojumulated away leaving the Baker to wonder and you to discover at *exactly* what time the Snark was given to dining (according to his watch) on the following day.


## Dr Asher gets down to it

At $x$ minutes past the hours the two main hands are 20 minutes (or 40 minutes) apart, and a third (snarked) hand registers $u$ seconds *ahead* of real time ($u$ stands for upgrading).

The problem is to find the smallest value of $u$.

Note: one eleventh of a minute $= 5\frac{5}{11}$ seconds. This value is constantly coming up in the calculations.

**A**

$12 \cdot 21\frac{9}{11}$

$x - \frac{1}{12}x = 20 \quad 11x = 240$

$x = 21\frac{9}{11} \quad \left(\frac{9}{11}\min = 49\frac{1}{11}\sec\right)$

**B**

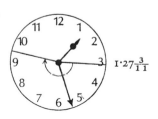

$12 \cdot 43\frac{7}{11}$

$x - \frac{1}{12}x = 40 \quad 11x = 480$

$x = 43\frac{7}{11} \quad \left(\frac{7}{11}\min = 38\frac{2}{11}\sec\right)$

**C**

$1 \cdot 27\frac{3}{11}$

$x - \left(5 + \frac{1}{12}x\right) = 20 \quad \frac{11}{12}x = 25$
$11x = 300$
$x = 27\frac{3}{11} \quad \left(\frac{3}{11}\min = 16\frac{4}{11}\sec\right)$

**D**

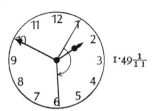

$1 \cdot 49\frac{1}{11}$

$x - \left(5 + \frac{1}{12}x\right) = 40 \quad \frac{11}{12}x = 45$
$11x = 540$
$x = 49\frac{1}{11} \quad \left(\frac{1}{11}\min = 5\frac{5}{11}\sec\right)$

E

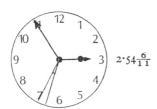

$$x - \left(10 + \tfrac{1}{12}x\right) = 20 \qquad \tfrac{11}{12}x = 30$$
$$11x = 360$$
$$x = 32\tfrac{8}{11} \quad \left(\tfrac{8}{11}\,\text{min} = 43\tfrac{7}{11}\,\text{sec}\right)$$

2·32$\tfrac{8}{11}$

F

$$x - \left(10 + \tfrac{1}{12}x\right) = 40 \qquad \tfrac{11}{12}x = 50$$
$$11x = 600$$
$$x = 54\tfrac{6}{11} \quad \left(\tfrac{6}{11}\,\text{min} = 32\tfrac{8}{11}\,\text{sec}\right)$$

2·54$\tfrac{6}{11}$

G

$$x - \left(15 + \tfrac{1}{12}x\right) = 20 \qquad \tfrac{11}{12}x = 35$$
$$11x = 420$$
$$x = 38\tfrac{2}{11} \quad \left(\tfrac{2}{11}\,\text{min} - 10\tfrac{10}{11}\,\text{sec}\right)$$

3.38$\tfrac{2}{11}$

H

4·00 o'clock   No calculation needed

I

$$x - \left(20 + \tfrac{1}{12}x\right) = 20 \qquad \tfrac{11}{12}x = 40$$
$$11x = 480$$
$$x = 43\tfrac{7}{11} \quad \left(\tfrac{7}{11}\,\text{min} = 38\tfrac{2}{11}\,\text{sec}\right)$$

4·43$\tfrac{7}{11}$

**J**

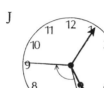

5·5$\frac{5}{11}$

$$(25+\tfrac{1}{12}x)-x = 20 \quad 1\tfrac{1}{12}x = 5$$
$$11x = 60 \quad x = 5\tfrac{5}{11}$$
$$(\tfrac{5}{11}\text{min} = 25\tfrac{25}{11}\text{sec} = 27\tfrac{3}{11}\text{sec})$$

**K**

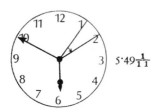

5·49$\frac{1}{11}$

$$x-(25+\tfrac{1}{12}x) = 20 \quad 1\tfrac{1}{12}x = 45$$
$$11x = 540$$
$$x = 49\tfrac{1}{11} \quad (\tfrac{1}{11}\text{min} = 5\tfrac{5}{11}\text{sec})$$

**L**

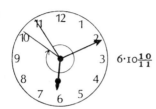

6·10$\frac{10}{11}$

$$30+\tfrac{1}{12}x-x = 20 \quad 1\tfrac{1}{12}x = 10$$
$$11x = 120$$
$$x = 10\tfrac{10}{11} \quad (\tfrac{10}{11}\text{min} = 54\tfrac{6}{11}\text{sec})$$

**M**

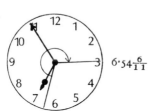

6·54$\frac{6}{11}$

$$x-(30+\tfrac{1}{12}x) = 20 \quad 1\tfrac{1}{12}x = 50$$
$$11x = 600$$
$$x = 54\tfrac{6}{11} \quad (\tfrac{6}{11}\text{min} = 32\tfrac{8}{11}\text{sec})$$

**N**

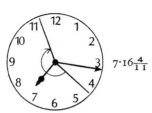

7·16$\frac{4}{11}$

$$35+\tfrac{1}{12}x-x = 20 \quad 1\tfrac{1}{12}x = 45$$
$$11x = 540$$
$$x = 16\tfrac{4}{11} \quad (\tfrac{4}{11}\text{min} = 21\tfrac{9}{11}\text{sec})$$

O

8 o'clock    No calculation needed

P

$8 \cdot 21\frac{9}{11}$

$$(40+\tfrac{x}{12})-x = 20 \quad \tfrac{11}{12}x = 20$$
$$11x = 240$$
$$x = 21\tfrac{9}{11} \quad (\tfrac{9}{11}\text{ min} = 49\tfrac{1}{11}\text{ sec})$$

Q

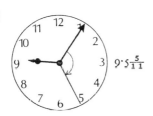

$9 \cdot 5\frac{5}{11}$

$$45+\tfrac{1}{12}x-x = 40 \quad \tfrac{11}{12}x = 5$$
$$11x = 60$$
$$x = 5\tfrac{5}{11} \quad (\tfrac{5}{11}\text{ min} - 5\tfrac{5}{11}\text{ sec})$$

R

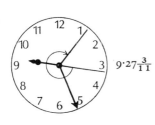

$9 \cdot 27\frac{3}{11}$

$$45+\tfrac{1}{12}x-x = 20 \quad \tfrac{11}{12}x = 25$$
$$11x = 300$$
$$x = 27\tfrac{3}{11} \quad (\tfrac{3}{11}\text{ min} = 16\tfrac{4}{11}\text{ sec})$$

S

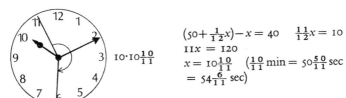

$10 \cdot 10\frac{10}{11}$

$$(50+\tfrac{1}{12}x)-x = 40 \quad \tfrac{11}{12}x = 10$$
$$11x = 120$$
$$x = 10\tfrac{10}{11} \quad (\tfrac{10}{11}\text{ min} = 50\tfrac{50}{11}\text{ sec}$$
$$= 54\tfrac{6}{11}\text{ sec})$$

T

$10\cdot32\frac{8}{11}$

$(50+\frac{1}{12}x)-x = 20 \quad \frac{11}{12}x = 30$

$11x = 360$

$x = 32\frac{8}{11} \quad \left(\frac{8}{11}\,\text{min} = 43\frac{7}{11}\,\text{sec}\right)$

U

$11\cdot16\frac{4}{11}$

$55+\frac{1}{12}x-x = 40 \quad \frac{11}{12}x = 15$

$11x = 180$

$x = 16\frac{4}{11} \quad \left(\frac{4}{11}\,\text{min} = 21\frac{9}{11}\,\text{sec}\right)$

V

$11\cdot38\frac{2}{11}$

$55+\frac{1}{12}x-x = 20 \quad \frac{11}{12}x = 35$

$11x = 426$

$x = 38\frac{2}{11} \quad \left(\frac{2}{11}\,\text{min} = 10\frac{10}{11}\,\text{sec}\right)$

W

$12\cdot21\frac{9}{11}$

But this is where we came in and no smaller value for $u$ has been found since example F.

ANSWER His watch shows the time as 5 minutes and $25\frac{5}{11}$ sec before 3 o'clock when the Snark dines (the actual time being nearly 2 seconds earlier as he pushed the second hand $1\frac{9}{11}$ seconds forward (see picture, p 97)).

# The Maker of Bonnets and Hoods to the Bellman

My Dear Bellman,

I heard only today that I had correctly found the Snark's dinner time, so I now enclose my calculations [see page 90] together with a presentation watch for yourself. I attach herewith the very pleasant letter from the author of the problem which you may wish to keep.

Yours ever

# Mr D St P Barnard to Dr Richard Asher

Dear Dr Asher,

Your letter of April 23rd concerning the Snark's dinner time seems to have got thoroughly "snarked up." In the first place, you seem to have directed it to *The Sunday Times* instead of *The Observer*[1] and in the second place, by the time it had reached me I had become the victim of rather a longish bout of illness from which I am now just recovering. My apologies therefore for the inordinate delay in answering your query.

In the first place, I agree entirely with your findings – viz, that the Snark dines at 2.54 and 34 6/11 seconds; and, in the second place, I see no other way of approaching the problem than that which you used, at least, the one I presume you used, which is to start at 4.00 and 8.00, add 1 1/11 hrs successively to each of these times to discover when hour and minute hands form an angle of 120°, and then to

---

[1] "Typical of R Asher!" [Comment from the Bellman of the Snark club].

calculate the times at which of these 22 occasions the second hand bisects the other two.

I was most interested to learn of the existence of the Snark club – Bellman and all. Surely with your bent for mathematics you qualify for the official post of Butcher for Fit The Fifth[1] (unless that post requires an FRCS instead of an FRCP).

Yours frabjously,

---

[1] So engrossed was the Butcher, he heeded them not,
    As he wrote with a pen in each hand,
    And explained all the while in a popular style
    Which the Beaver could well understand.

Taking Three as the subject to reason about –
A convenient number to state –
We add Seven, and Ten, and then multiply out
By One Thousand diminished by Eight.

The result we proceed to divide, as you see,
By Nine Hundred and Ninety and Two:
Then subtract Seventeen, and the answer must be
Exactly and perfectly true.

(The Hunting of the Snark, Fit the Fifth)

"Come, listen, my men, while I tell you again
The five unmistakable marks
By which you may know, wheresoever you go,
The warranted genuine Snarks."

(*The Hunting of the Snark*, Fit the Second)